BLEEDERSHIP

Biblical First – Aid for Leaders

JIM LANGE

TATE PUBLISHING, LLC

Acknowledgements

When thinking about who I should acknowledge in regard to this book, I realized that I need to first and foremost, thank God, my Father in heaven for placing the idea for this book on my heart while sitting in church in December, 2003. Thank you also to Pastor Glenn Teal for delivering that inspiring message from God. I also thank God for prodding me along, even when I did not feel overly enthused about continuing with this work.

Second, I need to thank my awesome wife, Connie who gave loving advice and was patient with me throughout the writing of this book. Without her support, encouragement and suggestions, there is no possible way that I would have finished.

In addition, thank you to my wonderful children, Kristin, Molly and Robbie who inspire me everyday. You are the best any father could ask for.

I would also like to thank those who have helped me greatly by reading this manuscript and offering their input and guidance: Robert Anders, Chris Bonham, John Broer, Terry Buske, Clark Conley, Bob Hedstrom, Laurie Keifer, Julie Lange, Sharon Lange, Pat McIntyre, Ed Reiter, Scott Taylor, Glenn Teal, Keith Walker and the wonderful people at Tate Publishing.

Finally, I would like to thank you, the reader of this book. I know that we all have choices in how we spend our resources and I sincerely appreciate your purchase of this book. Each of you possesses a different level of leadership ability. Whatever step you are on, my prayer for you is that this book touches your heart and inspires you to become more of a Biblical – type leader.

TABLE OF CONTENTS

FOREWORD

I had the honor and privilege to work with Jim Lange for nearly four years. During our professional time together, Jim was my mentor as a peer and eventually as my supervisor. Since Jim has left our company, one thought has been continually on my mind: "As one of the most spiritually–sound, ethically–centered, and most professional men I have ever known, how could we ever let Jim leave our company?"

While I continue to look for an answer to that question for selfish reasons, I understand that God has a plan for all of us, Jim included. As you read the book you are now holding, it may surprise you to learn that I am glad to have gone through the many professional challenges of which Jim speaks as it has taught me much.

Leadership is a God–given gift. While many of us live our lives without ever having identified our gifts, not to mention using these precious tools, Jim Lange is an example of an individual who welcomed the challenge to lead others.

While Jim's peer, I treasured his recommendations and often sought his counsel on important decisions that would affect my professional career as well as the future of my family. With Jim as my boss, I could not have asked for a stronger leader. Most importantly as a Christian, husband and father, I could not have had a better role model than the every–day example provided by Jim.

If I were reading this book without having witnessed the many things of which Jim speaks, I would find them far–fetched. I can assure you that these tests that God placed in front of Jim and all of us, did happen. It also struck me as I read this book that it may seem for those who don't know Jim, that he is a pushover. I can assure you, that is not the case. In fact, through the leadership and professional challenges Jim illustrates in this book, his faith and especially his witness to those he worked with, only increased.

I am confident that you will learn from and apply the Christian leadership lessons Jim has illustrated in this book. I hope you enjoy it as much as I have.

– Clark Conley

CHAPTER 1
HOW'D WE GET IN THIS MESS ANYWAY?

"A great attitude is not the result of success;
success is the result of a great attitude."
– Earl Nightingale

"Ability is what you're capable of doing. Motivation
determines what you do. Attitude determines how well you do it."
– Lou Holtz

"Any fact facing us is not as important as our attitude toward
it, for that determines our success or failure. The way you think
about a fact may defeat you before you ever do anything about
it. You are overcome by the fact because you think you are."
– Norman Vincent Peale

"Make education a continuing, never–ending process."
– Nido Qubein

"I wanted to change the world. But I have found that the
only thing one can be sure of changing is oneself."
– Aldous Huxley

A woman in a hot air balloon realized she was lost. She lowered her altitude and spotted a man below. She descended a bit more and shouted, "Excuse me, can you help me? I have no idea where I am and I promised a friend I would meet him an hour ago."

The man consulted his GPS monitor and replied, "You are in a hot air balloon approximately 30 feet above a ground elevation of 2,346 feet above sea level. You are 31 degrees, 14.97 minutes north latitude and 100 degrees, 49.09 minutes west longitude."

"You must be an engineer," said the balloonist.

"I am," replied the man. "How did you know?"

"Well," answered the balloonist, "everything you told me is technically correct, but I have no idea what to make of your information, and the fact is I am still lost. Frankly, you've not been much help so far."

The man responded, "You must be in management."

"I am," replied the balloonist, "but how did you know?"

"Well," said the man, "first, you don't know where you are or where you are going. Second, you have risen to where you are, due to a large quantity of hot air. Third, you made a promise you can't keep, and furthermore, you expect me, someone else, to solve your problems. The fact is, lady, you are in exactly the same position you were in before we met, but now somehow it is my fault."

I felt compelled to write this book as I have spent the past eighteen months working for a man who resembled the woman balloonist described above. I will call him "I.M. Boss." Prior to I.M. Boss's arrival, I was a sales representative who loved his job, worked very hard and made a nice living. I had been with the company for six years.

When I.M. Boss asked me to become the vice president of sales, my first reaction was to say "No thanks!" I then came to realize that this would be a wonderful experience for me that would allow me to grow in my career and give me some tremendous experience. So I accepted his offer. My role was to mentor our salespeople or "coach" them – to help them to be better producers.

At first, I thought very highly of I.M. Boss. He came into our company and made some changes in the first month that seemed very positive. Yes, he was a little arrogant and somewhat abrasive, but he was likeable and he kept telling us that we were going to have fun. I had no reason not to believe him.

We had nineteen people in our sales organization who reported to me which was a large number. Since most of them were experienced sales professionals, I did not feel the large number would be an issue, so I plowed ahead.

Two of our sales reps were selling into a market that was not of our core competency. Although this was a segment of business we were not familiar with, there was a lot of potential in this area. I.M. Boss came up with the idea that we needed to hire six additional sales people to take advantage of this opportunity. One of those hires would manage this area and presumably bring some experience to us in this vertical market.

We hired the manager of this group in December of that year and he was terrific. He not only knew the market, he was a very diligent worker, had a positive attitude and was a great team player. He would go out of his way to help me with any projects I had.

I.M. Boss had anticipated that it would take us until mid February to hire the remaining five sales people. It actually took us until August to complete this task because it was difficult to find solid people with the experience we were looking for. This coupled with the fact that I.M. Boss did not understand our business, led to much anxiety, as we were *not* producing at the level I.M. Boss had anticipated.

Because I.M. Boss was expecting such a high return from our new hires, and probably because of his ego, he signed us up for a huge growth goal with our corporate office. The year prior we had grown 6% and I.M. Boss told corporate we could do 25% this year. As the year progressed, we fell further and further behind.

This produced pressure from our corporate office. As this pressure intensified, I.M. Boss became more and more of a tyrant. We quickly began to see that we were in for a less than pleasant experience.

I considered leaving the company every day for the last eight months of my tenure there. I finally left in early 2004 and I feel that God was very much a part of that decision. I will not bore you with all the details, but one point toward the end of my decision – making process bears telling.

The Sunday after Christmas, 2003, my wife and I attended our usual home group meeting through our church. We completed our Bible study for the evening and our group leader suggested that we do something a little different. He said we were going to "pray over each other."

He pulled an ottoman out and asked who wanted to go first. That person told us what he wanted us to pray for and we placed our hands on him and prayed individual prayers aloud together. It was a very powerful experience.

I volunteered to go next. I stated that I was feeling led to quit my job but I wanted to make sure this was God's will and not my "taking the easy way out."

Everyone placed their hands on me and prayed. It was awesome!

I was on vacation the entire next week between Christmas and New Year's day. Monday morning as I was getting ready to leave for a doctor's appointment, I received a call from my assistant. I.M. Boss had requested that I be a part of a conference call that morning at 10:30. She said she tried to explain to him that I was on vacation, but he was adamant – I *must* be on the call. I reluctantly agreed to attend the call with no idea of the subject matter. Please keep in mind that I was not scheduled to be on this call.

The call started with I.M. Boss, four of our salespeople and me on the line. I.M. Boss began by attacking the salespeople. Then he began to attack me, telling me that I needed to be more prepared. When I tried to interject that I was not scheduled to be on this call and that I was on vacation, he blew up. He told all of us, "You all just got a plane ticket to our west coast office this Sunday (the last day of my vacation)! You need to get your %$#@ together between now and then so you can present to me at 8:00 Monday morning!"

After forty–five minutes of abuse I hung up the phone, looked to the heavens and said, "Okay God – I got it. I *am* supposed to leave the company!" God sure is awesome!

I *did* attend the meeting out west, which proved to be a disaster. We spent four hours simply listening to I.M. Boss scream at us about how worthless we were. This further confirmed my decision. I resigned the end of that week.

I do not want the message of this book to be one of bitterness toward I.M. Boss. I sincerely have no hard feelings. Rather than showing animosity toward him, I am eternally grateful for the opportunity he provided in allowing me to be his vice president of sales. I am also grateful for the education I received. In addition, I believe that God was using I.M. Boss to get my attention as my faith grew significantly during this time.

While there was tremendous pain felt by many people in our organization at the hands of I.M. Boss, I can honestly say that I am truly thankful that he entered my life. I actually feel blessed to have been associated with him, as I learned a lot from him – some of what *to* do and much of what *not* to do as a leader. It may seem hard to believe, but I actually like I.M. Boss.

EVERYTHING BUT A LEADER

I.M. Boss came to our company (a $150 million division of a $900 million publicly traded corporation) approximately two years ago as our new president. He came from a very large company in corporate America that was in an industry totally unrelated to ours. I guess our corporate big wigs thought that he could bring his "big company" knowledge to our "little company" even though he had no clue about our business.

What we all discovered was that his "big company" views really were nothing more than very selfish views of how *we* could serve *him.* His first day he shared with us "The 22 rules of I.M. Boss." These were a compilation of rules we had to follow to remain employed. The overall gist of these rules (I will share these rules in chapter 4) is that, I.M. Boss is king, we should bow down and worship him, and without him we would be bumbling idiots. Overall, it was a grand first impression!

Most companies use a "mission statement" when making company decisions. For example, let's assume that a company's mission statement is "to provide world class customer service." They would be more likely to spend money for a new phone system that would enable them to track and answer customer calls more timely since this would pass their "mission statement" test.

From the moment I.M. Boss walked into our lives, every one of our corporate decisions was not put through the "mission statement filter," but rather through the "I.M. Boss filter." The I.M. Boss filter would determine if this course of action would make I.M. Boss look good, make him more comfortable or would enhance his air of superiority. It was as if our mission statement had magically changed to: *Make I.M. Boss look good and enhance his standing with the corporate big guys at all costs.*

No one can argue that Jesus was the most gifted leader of all time. (In fact, He is still leading though He has not physically walked this earth for over 2000 years). We may have seen people who were great at *motivating,* great at *encouraging,* great at *telling us we need to work on some things,* and even some who were great at *speaking passionately* to a crowd. It is very rare however, to find someone who can do *all* of these things well and get his or her message across in a way that makes you want to believe the way Jesus did.

This book will guide you through the ways that many people in America lead and contrast that with the amazing way that Jesus and other Biblical leaders led more than 2,000 years ago. Though this book has many references to business, it is not just about leadership in the business setting. It will cover all types of leadership whether it be in business, leading your small group in your church, leading the little league team you

are coaching or leading your family – arguably the most important form of leadership today!

Throughout Scripture, Jesus and others teach us how to
lead. We need to be obedient, listen and follow His example.
I thank you with all of my heart for purchasing this book. My
prayer is that we can all "learn me his experience" as Yogi Berra
used to say. I hope you enjoy!

CHAPTER 2
HUMBLE LEADERSHIP

"It takes humility to seek feedback. It takes wisdom to
understand it, analyze it, and appropriately act on it."
– Stephen Covey

"You can accomplish anything in life, provided
that you do not mind who gets the credit."
– Harry Truman

"A talented trumpeter who toots his own horn winds up
playing to an empty theatre. A talented trumpeter who
lets others recognize his talent winds up a legend."
– Lisa Edmondson

"We grow small trying to be great."
– E. Stanley Jones

"A winner is big enough to admit his mistakes, smart enough
to profit from them and strong enough to correct them."
– John Maxwell

"The truth is that there is nothing noble in being
superior to somebody else. The only real
nobility is in being superior to your former self."
– Whitney Young

THE GUY IN THE GLASS

When you get what you want in your struggle for pelf*,
And the world makes you King for a day,
Then go to the mirror and look at yourself,
And see what that guy has to say.

For it isn't your Father, or Mother, or Wife,
Whose judgment upon you must pass.
The feller whose verdict counts most in your life
Is the guy staring back from the glass.

He's the feller to please, never mind all the rest,
For he's with you clear up to the end,
And you've passed your most dangerous, difficult test
If the guy in the glass is your friend.

You may be like Jack Horner and "chisel" a plum,
And think you're a wonderful guy,
But the man in the glass says you're only a bum
If you can't look him straight in the eye.

You can fool the whole world down the pathway of years,
And get pats on the back as you pass,
But your final reward will be heartaches and tears
If you've cheated the guy in the glass.

– Dale Wimbrow

*pelf is a derogatory word for money or wealth. (Oxford Dictionary)

It is unfortunate, but after talking with many business people, I have to say that most so called "leaders" in corporate America have a very "puffed up" sense of themselves.

Let's face it. Not everyone is willing to do the things necessary to be a leader. I suppose that because of this fact, many of those who lead think that puts them a step above the rest of the working class.

Many of these individuals have obtained their knowledge by going to school. My boss got a "degree" from the Harvard School of Business and never passed up an opportunity to remind us of his Harvard "MBA." We later learned, however, that this was a four–week course he had taken while working for a company who paid his way.

Some leaders learn on the job. Some leaders have not learned at all and move up the ladder anyway. Do you know some of these people?

In any event, many corporate leaders feel a sense of "entitlement." What is good for them is good for the business. Don't we need our leaders to be well rested, in the most comfortable leather chairs, with the best flat screen computer monitors, in the corner office with the best view, driving the most expensive company cars? After all, our future and our very existence depends on their brilliant minds and leadership skills. They feel that if they are not fresh and well rested, well, we can just kiss our careers goodbye since we certainly could not accomplish anything without them!

As a result, we are stuck with people in leadership roles who are proud and arrogant. Needless to say, my boss insisted on having the best office, the best office furniture, the latest toys (handhelds that can receive emails while traveling, etc . . .) to the most expensive cars. He felt he deserved and was entitled to this simply because he was our leader.

I.M. Boss even refused to go on sales calls unless he was going to be used as the "closer" at the end of the sales process. He acted as if making calls early in the process was totally beneath him. Yet, when we would land a big sale, I.M. Boss would make sure to tell everyone that *he* was responsible for luring this client to us.

I.M. Boss would continually tell us that he was with our company because he saw himself as a college professor in that he had an opportunity to "teach" all of us. But instead of being paid like a professor, he got the bonus of being paid buckets of money. (Little did he know that he truly was teaching us a lot; how *NOT* to lead!) The following is something he actually told me,

"I know what the problem is between you and me. Do you want to hear it? I have been assuming you have different learnings [sic]. I have much more learnings [sic] than you. You don't know but I know you want to know. I have the magic and I need to share it with you."

In one instance, I.M. Boss asked me about our sales methodology with a particular client. He proceeded to tell me I did not have a "strategy." I told him that I used a particular sales process (that was documented as extremely successful over the years) and that is what we are teaching our sales organization. I.M. Boss said I should change *my* tactics and listen to <u>his</u> seventeen years of business experience (even though he has never sold anything before). He said, "Jim, I know you don't like my tactics and I know you don't like me, but I don't care – this is my house and we will do things my way!"

I.M. Boss really wanted me to be like him. He wanted me to yell and scream at the people on my team. The following is how one conversation went:

"You need to yell at them to make them respect you!

They are %&$#ing on both of us and it's going to get us fired. There is something fundamentally wrong when a piece of %&$# like Fred will survive and we won't! We are better than him!"

- He would tell us on numerous occasions that our job was simply "to make him look good."

- He would pull sales people on my team and me out of client meetings to help him work on presentations to his boss. Remember, making him look good was our unofficial company mission.

- He once told a female employee, "I need to be careful to avoid an affair since I am such a good looking guy."

- After meeting with a client for the first time, I.M. Boss asked the sales rep, "Do you think they liked me?" It was as if he felt the meeting was all about him.

- I.M. Boss would say to me quite often, "I love to eat the weak!"

He sounds like a peach of a guy, huh? My guess is that each of you is working for or has worked for someone like this, or you know someone who has. If you are currently in that situation, my heart goes out to you but I encourage you to be strong and to show others how to lead by your example.

In his arrogance the wicked man hunts down the weak,
who are caught in the schemes he devises.

(Psalm 10:2)

A BIBLICAL EXAMPLE

In the book of Esther we are introduced to another leader who is consumed with trying to gain respect simply due to his position. His name is Haman. Haman is placed in a position of power by King Xerxes in chapter 3. Because a "lesser" man named Mordecai would not bow down and worship him, Haman was deeply angered.

In Esther 5:9, Haman runs into Mordecai in the streets and when Mordecai does not even pay attention to him, Haman is burning with anger. He heads home to whine to his wife about this *lowlife* who will not pay him the respect he deserves.

His wife and his friends tell him to build a gallows and to hang Mordecai so he won't be a thorn in Haman's side anymore. (Do you suppose they may have been tired of hearing about this guy and they just wanted Haman's whining to stop?)

At the same time, the king was looking through the history books of his reign and discovered that Mordecai had uncovered a plot to kill the king. So Mordecai had actually saved King Xerxes' life.

The next day, Haman came to King Xerxes to tell him of his idea to have Mordecai killed. Before he could expose his plot, the king said that Mordecai should be honored for his deeds.

Haman was eventually hanged on the very gallows he had built to kill Mordecai. Does the saying "what goes around, comes around" come to mind? I guess this is a great example of what happens to those with pride.

The Lord detests all the proud of heart. Be sure of this,
they will not go unpunished.

(Proverbs 16:5)

JESUS' HUMBLE LEADERSHIP

Let's go back to Jesus' birth. God has total control of everything, right? Then why wasn't Jesus born in the grandest, most elaborate palace in a gold bassinet with a platinum spoon in His mouth?

Instead, Joseph and Mary were refused at the Inn so Jesus was born in the humblest of surroundings, a stable amongst cow dung. No pressed sheets, no hot water. Do you think that was an accident? I don't. I believe God had every intention of allowing Jesus to come from a lowly beginning.

The Jews were very excited about the thought of a monarch sent from God to free them from Roman oppression. Even though the early prophets said that the Savior would come as a servant, many did not think that this Messiah could come from such humble beginnings. So they missed it.

I think a lot of us are under the assumption that Jesus was not like normal babies since the usual union between a man and a woman did not conceive Him. In addition, the Bible doesn't discuss His childhood much (Luke 2:39–40). The only thing really talked about was that at age twelve He preached in the Temple for three days when His parents mistakenly left Him behind. We see that as abnormal, and we therefore assume that *nothing* was normal about Him. However, let me assure you, Jesus cried. He soiled His diapers. He burped. He fell and skinned His knees. He was just like us. Jesus did not take any shortcuts. He was not isolated from the temptations, pressures and the pain of life.

Jesus experienced all that we could possibly experience and then some. Hopefully, none of us will ever endure the pain and suffering that Jesus suffered.

God orchestrated this on purpose. He knew that the best leader would have to be *humble.*

Ponder this question: Don't you respect and listen to people who have been through the battles and can understand what you are feeling? Don't we discount leaders who really have never been in our shoes – who haven't experienced what we have experienced? Those who have been in the trenches and remember those experiences are usually much more effective as leaders.

Let's take stock of some of Jesus' attributes:

- Jesus was born in a stable – the most humble of beginnings.

- Jesus washed His disciples' feet the night before He was to be crucified. He did not ask for pity or for His disciples to serve Him.

- Jesus did not need to yell to gain respect or to get people to listen to Him. He never refused to help anyone – never thought anyone was beneath Him (in fact His disciples questioned why He would even help some people who were different).

- Jesus did not ask for the best of anything. He knew He was here to serve God and to teach others how to be humble. *Blessed are the poor in spirit, for theirs is the kingdom of heaven.* (Matthew 5:3).

- Jesus gave all credit to God – He took no credit for Himself. He helped all people – no one was beneath Him. (He even asked a lowly, dishonest tax collector to be one of His followers). The Book of Luke is filled with examples of Jesus' healing – all done without flash, with complete humility. He did not want the credit, as the healing came from God. In teaching, He did it humbly, not like He was above anyone. He understood His pupils and their faults. He commanded respect because of His compassion.

- Jesus never gloated or asked for approval. In fact, after one of His miracles, Jesus actually retreated to be by Himself rather than let the people congratulate Him. (John 6:15)

24

- Jesus never cared how He appeared. He looked like everyone else – no fancy clothes or shoes; just a robe and sandals.

Is this what you imagine from the greatest leader that ever lived?

PREPARATIONS FOR LEADERSHIP

Do you remember the story about Joseph? He was the guy whose father, Jacob, considered to be his favorite son. Because of this, Jacob gave Joseph a beautiful, richly adorned robe to wear. Joseph was so proud that he wore it at all times. Joseph was very full of himself.

Joseph's conceit so angered his eleven brothers that they actually considered killing him. Instead, they sold him into slavery to Potiphar, one of Pharoah's officials. Potiphar saw that the Lord was with Joseph. Everything Joseph did, he did well so Potiphar promoted him up the ladder until he was put in charge of Potiphar's household.

Joseph, being a "studly," well–built hunk, caught the eye of Potiphar's wife. She continually tried to seduce him. Joseph always resisted and remained faithful to his master and to God. This obviously frustrated Potiphar's wife, who I imagine, got what she wanted most of the time.

One day, when all of the servants were conveniently gone, Potiphar's wife cornered Joseph and made her move. Joseph escaped her advances but not before she grabbed his cloak. I imagine that she was furious! She proceeded to tell Potiphar that Joseph tried to rape her so Joseph was placed in jail. Rather than being angry and feeling sorry for himself, Joseph continued to humble himself before the Lord, and God continued to look favorably upon him.

Scripture states that after spending over two years in jail, Joseph was released and eventually became second in command to Pharaoh. What a turnaround! I believe this all happened because Joseph simply humbled himself before God and turned from his conceited ways.

Many of us may ask why God would treat Joseph that way. Why did he have to spend those years in jail even though he was falsely accused of the crime? I believe that God wanted Joseph to learn *humility*. He could not afford to have a prideful young man be the leader of one of the most powerful areas of His world.

Another great example of God's preparing someone for an important leadership role is the story of Moses.

By faith Moses, when he had grown up, refused to be known as the son of Pharaoh's daughter. He chose to be mistreated along with the people of God rather than to enjoy the pleasures of sin for a short time. He regarded disgrace for the sake of Christ as of greater value than the treasures of Egypt, because he was looking ahead to his reward.

(Hebrews 11:24–26)

Moses fled because Pharaoh was trying to kill him. Moses became a shepherd and lived as an unknown foreigner in a strange land. Keep in mind that he became a shepherd – a job that was detested by his financially privileged family. I suspect he could have used his name and upbringing to gain privileges but he chose the humble route. Moses refused to be treated better than other people. I find this remarkable.

That is the same as a Major League all–star baseball player choosing to become a batboy! Imagine Barry Bonds saying "I don't want to be paid millions of dollars anymore. I don't want fans applauding me anymore. I don't want to be on ESPN's SportsCenter anymore. I don't want to sign any more autographs. I think I will be a batboy instead."

He actually would not want anyone to know that he was the one picking up each player's bat and keeping the dugout clean. You see he wouldn't want any special favors done for him simply because of his name and status. This is pretty hard to imagine isn't it? Do you think you could do that?

Another interesting sidebar: during those dark times in our lives – could it be that God is preparing us for something? Those who have walked in dark valleys immediately have a kinship with those who have walked or are currently walking through hard places – they have a mutual respect and understanding of one another. So, perhaps our hardships occur to humble us and prepare us so that we can be a more effective leader.

Little did Moses know that during this dark time in his life, God was actually preparing him for a very important leadership position.

The stories of Joseph and Moses point out something very important for those of us who have been called to be a leader in our workplace, in our church or in our homes. God wants us to be humble prior to leading, during leading and after leading; in other words, at all times.

MIKE OR BETH?

Suppose, at your workplace you have two coworkers whom you interact with on a regular basis, Mike and Beth.

Mike works extremely hard. He is an enormous help to you as he takes a lot of the load off your shoulders because of his work ethic. The problem with Mike is that he thinks he is better than the rest of his coworkers. In fact, he is downright arrogant.

With every project, Mike is quick to take the credit for any successes and quick to blame others for anything less than a success.

While Beth does not get as much accomplished in a day as Mike, she is still a hard worker. When working on a project, Beth is very cognizant of her other team members. Given the opportunity, Beth gives all of the credit for successes to her teammates. She even accepts the blame for a project's shortcomings rather than blame her coworkers.

Mike and Beth are both up for a promotion to be the leader of your department. Mike clearly produces at a higher level than Beth. Who do you think should get the job? Which one of these individuals would *you* rather work for?

Most people would say Beth would be their choice and my guess is that Beth *would* be the better leader as she would build up her team and deflect any positive attention to her group. Don't you like it when your boss gives the credit to you?

On a bicycle, is one tire more important than the other? Some might say the back wheel is because that is where the power is. Others might say the front, because that is where the direction is controlled. However, both are very important and cannot work properly without the other. The same is true for the leader and his or her team.

Why don't we try to get our pride out of the way and give others credit even if we did most of the work? You know what? Everyone knows who did it anyway. We don't need to remind them.

═══════════════════════════

*Finally, all of you, live in harmony with one another;
be sympathetic, love as brothers, be compassionate
and humble.*

1 Peter 3:8

*Young men, in the same way be submissive to those who
are older. All of you, clothe yourselves with humility
toward one another, because, "God opposes the proud
but gives grace to the humble."*

1 Peter 5:5

*Seek the Lord, all you humble of the land, you who do what
he commands. Seek righteousness, seek humility; perhaps
you will be sheltered on the day of the Lord's anger.*

Zephaniah 1:17

*Do nothing out of selfish ambition or vain conceit, but in
humility consider others better than yourselves.*

Philippians 2:3

*Therefore, as God's chosen people, holy and dearly loved,
clothe yourselves with compassion, kindness, humility,
gentleness and patience.*

Colossians 3:12

*Remind the people to be subject to rulers and authorities,
to be obedient, to be ready to do whatever is good, to
slander no one, to be peaceable and considerate, and to
show true humility toward all men.*

Titus 3:1–2

*Now Moses was a very humble man, more humble than
anyone else on the face of the earth.*

Numbers 12:3

*But Moses said to God, "Who am I, that I should go to
Pharaoh and bring the Israelites out of Egypt?"*

Exodus 3:11

Do not keep talking so proudly or let your mouth speak such arrogance, for the Lord is a God who knows, and by him deeds are weighed.

1 Samuel 2:3

For in his own eyes he flatters himself too much to detect or hate sin. The words of his mouth are wicked and deceitful; he has ceased to be wise and to do good.

Psalm 36:2–3

CHAPTER 3
COMPASSIONATE
LEADERSHIP

"If you want others to be happy, practice
compassion. If you want to be happy, practice compassion."
– The Dali Lama

"Few things in the world are more powerful than
a positive push – a smile. A word of optimism and
hope, a 'you can do it!' when things are tough."
– Richard DeVos

"Nothing else can quite substitute for a few
well–chosen, well timed, sincere words of praise.
They're absolutely free – and worth a fortune."
– Sam Walton

"Kindness is the language which the deaf
can hear and the blind can see."
– Mark Twain

"There are two ways of exerting one's strength:
one is pushing down, the other is pulling up."
– Booker T. Washington

One day, a poor boy who was selling goods from door to door to pay his way through school, found he had only one thin dime left, and he was hungry.

He decided he would ask for a meal at the next house. However, he lost his nerve when a lovely young woman opened the door.

Instead of a meal, he asked for a drink of water. She thought he looked hungry so she brought him a large glass of milk. He drank it slowly, and then asked, "How much do I owe you?"

You don't owe me anything," she replied. "Mother has taught us never to accept pay for a kindness."

He said, "Then I thank you from my heart."

As Howard Kelly left that house, he not only felt stronger physically, but his faith in God and in mankind was stronger also. He had been ready to give up and quit.

Many years later that same young woman became critically ill. The local doctors were baffled. They finally sent her to the big city, where they called in specialists to study her rare disease.

Dr. Howard Kelly was called in for the consultation. When he heard the name of the town she came from, a strange light filled his eyes.

Immediately he rose and went down the hall to her room.

Dressed in his doctor's gown he went in to see her. He recognized her at once.

He went back to the consultation room determined to do his best to save her life. He gave special attention to her case and after a long struggle, the battle was won.

Dr. Kelly requested that the business office give the final bill to him for approval. He looked at it, then wrote something on the edge and the bill was sent to her room. She feared opening it, for she was sure it would take the rest of her life to pay for it all. Finally she looked, and something caught her attention on the side of the bill. She read these words . . .

"Paid in full with one glass of milk"

(Signed) Dr. Howard Kelly.

Tears of joy flooded her eyes and she prayed: "Thank You, God, that Your love has spread through human hearts and hands."

There's a saying which goes something like this:

Bread cast on the waters comes back to you. The good deed you do today may benefit you or someone you love at the least expected time. If you never see the deed again at least you will have made the world a better place – And, after all, isn't that what life is all about?

_____

"You will do it my way or I will have to kill you!" That is a command I would hear several times per week. No, I was not engaged in a battle in war. I was not a hostage listening to my kidnappers. I was simply in my office trying to do my job. "Kill" was I.M. Boss's way of saying "fire."

Because of the feeling of entitlement discussed in the previous chapter, many leaders feel they no longer need to be compassionate toward those who work for them. We see it regularly on ESPN where a star baseball, football or basketball player treats people poorly and is still revered as a king.

Even when these "stars" are involved in a court case and are accused of doing grievous harm to another, what usually happens? The media goes crazy and actually makes the person out to be some sort of a hero. I suppose it could be easy for these people to feel they no longer need to treat people with compassion. No matter what they do they are worshiped. It seems that the worse they behave the more they get the spotlight!

The same holds true of many of our leaders today outside of the sports world. No, they don't have cameras following their every move, but within the walls of their "kingdom" (office, home, playing field, etc.), they are looked at as the one in charge. This can go to a leader's head if he/she is not careful.

One day I.M. Boss decided that he wanted to improve the bottom line so he would look better to the corporate office. He decided that we needed to randomly cut $1 million in payroll from our company and the majority of the people to be affected would come from the sales organization. He told me that we needed to cut ten sales people.

We did indeed have a reduction in force. I.M. Boss later asked our top performing sales person what he thought of the reduction. He said, "I don't like it. Everyone is now looking over their shoulder wondering if they are next." I.M. Boss said, "Well, that is a good thing isn't it?" He obviously believed in the adage, "The beatings will continue until morale improves."

Here is another instance of motivational brilliance by our fearless leader. We had just hired six salespeople over the past six months to sell into a new niche for us. A couple of these had only been with our company for four weeks. These were all highly skilled professionals from our industry, yet anytime a new concept is introduced, it generally takes at least twelve to eighteen months to see results from your efforts – even with solid people in your sales organization, which I believe we had.

I.M. Boss did not understand this. He felt that this group should have been bringing on more business than our production facility could handle – immediately. He came to me on a Tuesday afternoon and said, "Jim, we don't have a strategy with this group. I want them all here tomorrow morning for a strategy session!"

I said, "I.M. Boss, they are all in the field making sales calls and two of our guys are on the west coast. They will have to fly all night to get here."

He replied, "I don't give a &%#@ about them! Get them in here no matter what!"

I said, "Joe is leaving on vacation so he won't be able to make it."

I.M. Boss said, "Tell Joe, I don't give a %$#@ about him or his vacation! If he wants a job, he will be here tomorrow!"

I proceeded to call everyone to our office. Two of the sales people took red–eye flights at a cost to the company of over $2,000. Joe had to postpone his vacation.

Before the meeting, I.M. Boss called me into his office to tell me that I needed to yell and scream at these people or they would not respect me (now there is a real nugget of wisdom). I told him I was not willing to do that. He completely blew up and announced that *he* would run the meeting.

I.M. Boss began the meeting and told the team they were the worst group of salespeople he had ever seen. He said they had better start bringing business on fast or they would all be gone. He then proceeded to write everyone's salary and commission on the white board. He wanted to make the point that the company is paying them lots of money and they haven't paid for themselves yet with new business. He pointed out that they were killing his profit numbers and costing *him* bonus dollars because of their horrendous performance.

When the sales people complained about his sharing of their compensation, I.M. Boss replied, "Well, they do it in professional sports so it should be no different here."

He continued with his "pep talk" in this vein for about an hour and then turned it over to me. Needless to say we were not inspired. Many athletes talk about running through brick walls for their coaches after a motivational talk. Our group probably could not have run through a wet paper bag! The group was less than motivated!

LEAD WITH COMPASSION

I once heard that anger is like the warning lights on your car's dashboard. They tell you that something is going on under the hood and you need to find out what is the source of the problem.

Rick Warren, in *The Purpose Driven Life* states "Only secure people can serve. Insecure people are always worrying about how they appear to others. They fear exposure of their weaknesses and hide beneath layers of protective pride and pretensions. The more insecure you are, the more you will want people to serve you, and the more you will need their approval."

Webster's says that insecurity is " . . . *a feeling of no confidence, filled with anxieties and apprehensiveness.*" Insecurity can lead to a need to control people and circumstances. This need to control can only lead to anger when things inevitably do not turn out exactly as we would like. In business, this typically leads to the employees becoming fearful of making wrong decisions. Their only motivation is to please the boss, as they know they could lose their jobs in an instant if they don't. This can result in a build up of resentment within the employees, which usually means they will have a total lack of respect for their leader.

As a side note, insecurity will inevitably lead to listening to, and trying to please our critics. Worrying about what others think of us will lead to making decisions based on a warped sense of what is right. This further deteriorates any respect a leader has.

When you look at the life of Jesus, He knew beyond a shadow of a doubt what His purpose was. He had no anxieties or apprehensiveness. He was as compassionate a leader as anyone who walked this earth. Did this attract followers? You bet it did! Could you imagine someone today walking into your place of work or your home and asking you to give up everything: your family, your job, your possessions, and your friends? All for what? To follow him and to be persecuted with no monetary pay?

That is exactly what Jesus did. In fact, He actually convinced twelve people to follow Him and to give up everything they had. How did He do this? I believe it was, in part, due to His tremendous compassion. Have you ever heard the saying "people will not care how much you know until they know how much you care?" That was certainly true of Jesus and His followers. They knew that He cared deeply for them.

Think about the best teachers you had in school. My guess is that they were the most compassionate ones. How about the best coach you ever had? Again, probably the most compassionate. How about the best boss you have ever had? Do you get the point?

People do not care how much you know until they know how much you care!

Let's look at a day when Jesus was both rejoicing with His apostles and mourning the loss of a dear friend. In Mark 6 Jesus says *"Come with me by yourselves to a quiet place to get some rest."* He wanted to go someplace quiet to relax with His disciples so He could hear about what they had been doing and to celebrate with them. In addition, He had just learned of the death of John the Baptist so He probably wanted some solitude to mourn for His dear friend and relative.

He took the disciples by boat to a place of solitude for some quiet fellowship. He didn't anticipate that the throng of people who were following Him would go ahead of them and be waiting for Him when He arrived. Instead of arriving at a quiet place and having some downtime with His pals, He was greeted by a large crowd who wanted more of Him.

How would you handle a situation like this? Would you be happy to see everyone and embrace the situation or would you likely be angry and want to escape? I know I would probably not handle this well. I would more than likely storm off with my friends so I could relax. But what did Jesus do?

Mark 6:34 says, *When Jesus landed and saw a large crowd, he had compassion on them, because they were like sheep without a shepherd. So he began teaching them many things.*

His disciples then came to Him and said, *"Send the people away so they can go to the surrounding countryside and villages and buy themselves something to eat."*

Jesus said, *"Give them something to eat."*

As we know, the disciples complained that it would take *"eight months of a man's wages"* to feed this many people. Jesus took what He had, five loaves and two fish, and fed all the people.

The miracle in food multiplication is incredible but

another point I think is amazing is how Jesus "*had compassion on them.*" His plans for relaxation and mourning John the Baptist were not only ruined by these demanding people, He also had to feed all of them! What freeloaders! But He did it with love and compassion.

Throughout the Gospels, we see examples of Jesus' compassion, especially when He is healing people. *Jesus had compassion on them and touched their eyes. Immediately they received their sight and followed him.* (Matthew 20:34) ... *he had compassion on them and healed their sick.* (Matthew 14:14)

How many of us actually run the other way when someone has a need, especially someone we lead? How about when we are really stressed? Our attitudes oftentimes are, "they can handle it – I've got to stay focused so I can get *my* stuff done!"

Who would you rather follow, someone who cares about you as a human being or a tyrant who just sees you as employee number 317? Dale Carnegie said that you will influence a lot more people in a shorter amount of time by showing an interest in them than by constantly telling them about yourself and your ideas.

Jesus always looked at (and still looks at) people through rose–colored glasses. What I mean by this is that He always viewed people in the best possible light, for who they could become rather than who they were. He still sees the best in all of us. He understands what we have been through. Shouldn't we be the same way?

==

I received this by email from a friend of mine and I would like to offer this prayer to you as a leader. Please remember that everyone needs compassion.

Heavenly Father,

Help us remember that the idiot who cut us off in traffic last night is a single mother who worked nine hours that day and is rushing home to cook dinner, help with homework, do the laundry and spend a few precious moments with her children.

Help us to remember that the pierced, tattooed, disinterested young man who can't make change correctly is a worried 19–year–old college student balancing his apprehension over final exams with his fear of not getting his student loans for next semester.

Remind us Lord, that the scary looking bum, begging for money in the same spot every day (who really ought to get a job!) is a slave to addictions that we can only imagine in our worst nightmares.

Help us to remember that the old couple walking annoyingly slow through the store aisles and blocking our shopping progress is savoring this moment, knowing that, based on the biopsy report she got back last week, this will be the last year they go shopping together.

Heavenly Father, remind us each day that, of all the gifts you give us, the greatest gift is love. It is not enough to share that love with those we hold dear. Open our hearts not to just those who are close to us, but to all humanity.

Let us judge not lest we be judged; let us be quick to forgive and let us show patience, empathy and love. Amen.

Matthew 10:30 tells us that God cares so much about us that he even knows how many hairs are on our head! Don't you think we, as leaders should at least show compassion to our followers?

ROBERT OR LARRY?

Robert is a co–worker of yours and he is always willing to listen to you. He doesn't seem to judge you even though you could easily be judged. He always seems to know when to give you a word of encouragement. He works hard and does his job well.

Larry, also one of your teammates, is an extremely hard worker and the top producer in your division. It seems that he never has time to talk about anything because he is so driven to produce.

Both of them are the finalists for a promotion to run your department. Will Larry, the top producer help to motivate everyone to produce at his level? Or will Robert help to show your department that each of them is important and thus spur them on to greater things?

If I had to bet, based on my experience and the experience of many I know, Robert would be the winner. Compassion will win out over a hard–driving, non–personal leadership style. It is certainly possible that Larry could change his ways once he started his new position. He would need to do that and become more compassionate if he wants the success he desires.

Remember, people don't *care* how much you *know,* until they *know* how much you *care.*

If I speak in tongues of men and of angels, but have not love, I am only a resounding gong or a clanging cymbal. If I have the gift of prophecy and can fathom all mysteries and all knowledge, and if I have faith that can move mountains, but have not love, I am nothing. If I give all I possess to the poor and surrender my body to the flames, but have not love, I gain nothing.

1 Corinthians 13:1 – 3

Be kind and compassionate to one another, forgiving each other, just as in Christ God forgave you.

Ephesians 4:32

Therefore, as God's chosen people, holy and dearly loved, clothe yourselves with compassion, kindness, humility, gentleness and patience.

Colossians 3:12

Finally, all of you, live in harmony with one another; be sympathetic, love as brothers, be compassionate and humble.

1 Peter 3:8

CHAPTER 4
SERVANT LEADERSHIP

"It is one of the most beautiful compensations of life, that no man can sincerely try to help another without helping himself."
– Ralph Waldo Emerson

"Don't be reluctant to give of yourself generously, it's the mark of caring and compassion and personal greatness."
– Brian Tracy

"The charity that is a trifle to us can be precious to others."
– Homer

"We make a living by what we get, but we make a life by what we give."
– Norman MacEwan

"Courtesies of a small and trivial character are the ones which strike deepest in the grateful and appreciating heart."
– Henry Clay

"The greatest use of life is to spend it for something that will outlast it."
– William James

A small boy is sent to bed by his father.

Five minutes later…

"Da–ad …"

"What?"

"I'm thirsty. Can you come bring me a drink of water?"

"No. You had your chance. Lights out."

Five minutes later…

"Da–aaaad …"

"WHAT?"

"I'm THIRSTY. Can I have a drink of water?"

"I told you NO! If you ask again, I'll have to spank you!!"

Five minutes later …

"Daaaaaa–aaaaaad …"

"WHAT!"

"When you come to spank me, can you bring me a drink of water?"

———————————————————

On I.M. Boss's first day at our company he passed out his "22 Rules." If we would follow these we would have no problems, he told us. The following are a list of his rules:

1) THE CUSTOMER IS KING

• Headquarters and the Plant live for the Customer

2) LOYALTY IS EVERYTHING

- It is a foundation of life

- Once you leave the boss's office it is your problem

- Take responsibility – don't blame the boss

3) TIMING IS SECOND ONLY TO LOYALTY

4) THE BOSS IS NUMBER ONE, TWO AND THREE

- Find out his/her hot buttons

- After you get direction, don't try to negotiate him/her down

- Just do it

- Realize that he/she has all the power in the relationship

5) BE PROACTIVE ALMOST TO A FAULT

- Do not wait for someone else to fix your problems

6) WHEN YOU PRESENT A PROBLEM: NAMES, DATES AND ACTION ITEMS

- State the problem

- Give the boss an action program in outline form

  ❧Who is responsible?

  ❧What they are to do, when will they start, when will they be finished?

7) DON'T MISS DATES OF KEY ACTION ITEMS

8) DON'T BE LATE TO MEETINGS

9) PUT THE COMPANY FIRST

- If it's good for the company it's good for your career

- Run your desk like it is your company

10) NO SURPRISES

- Don't be afraid to deliver bad news, but deliver a corrective action plan with it

- Bad news is not wine – it does not improve with age

11) DRAGNET'S DETECTIVE JOE FRIDAY – "Just the Facts Ma'am."

- Up front

- Blunt

- Candid

12) COMMUNICATIONS

- No one has ever over–communicated themselves out of a job

13) GOALS: BE RELENTLESS, DOGMATIC, INTENSE AND UNCOMPROMISING

- Early to bed, early to rise, work real hard, then advertise

14) SHARE THE GLORY – "They" know who did most of it

15) NO SECOND CHANCE TO MAKE A FIRST IMPRESSION

16) GET ALL THE LIARS IN THE SAME ROOM

17) ALWAYS TELL THE TRUTH (DO NOT LIE, CHEAT OR STEAL)

18) NEVER MAKE A CAREER DECISION BASED SOLELY ON YOUR PRESENT BOSS

19) VIEWS ON MANAGEMENT:

- Managers are in charge – all the authority one has, has been delegated to them by their boss

- The more comfortable the boss feels, the more power a person is given

- Managers choose which problems to live with

- Run the department so the best people love it

- Management sits in the grandstand when times are good

20) ELIMINATE ROADBLOCKS AND EXCUSES – PERCEIVED OR REAL

21) WALK THE TALK

22) HAVE FUN – or find a job or organization that can give it to you

---

Now, on the surface these rules sound pretty good; however, we later found that these rules *actually* were as follows:

1) THE CUSTOMER IS KING

- I (I.M. Boss) am your customer/king – you must bow to me and serve me

2) LOYALTY IS EVERYTHING

- You must be loyal to me at all times no matter what

3) TIMING IS SECOND ONLY TO LOYALTY

- You cannot do anything until I say the timing is right

4) THE BOSS IS NUMBER ONE, TWO AND THREE

- I am wonderful

5) BE PROACTIVE ALMOST TO A FAULT

- Do everything for me so that I can get the glory (and the cash)

6) WHEN YOU PRESENT A PROBLEM: NAMES, DATES AND ACTION ITEMS

- My time is too valuable to be wasting it with you

7) DON'T MISS DATES OF KEY ACTION ITEMS

- Or I will show you how powerful I am

8) DON'T BE LATE TO MEETINGS

- I will always be late to meetings but you never can – see rule # 1, 3, 4

9) PUT THE COMPANY FIRST

- This only sounds good – you must put me first, then the company will prosper

10) NO SURPRISES

- Never surprise me with bad news, only good news

- I can not lose focus on how wonderful I am – bad news makes me lose focus

11) DRAGNET'S DETECTIVE JOE FRIDAY – "Just the Facts Ma'am."

- See rule #6

12) COMMUNICATIONS

- You must tell me how wonderful I am at least six times per day

13) GOALS: BE RELENTLESS, DOGMATIC, INTENSE AND UNCOMPROMISING

- Goal #1: you live for me

- Goal #2: see goal #1

- Goal #3: see goal #2

14) SHARE THE GLORY

- You shouldn't take all of the credit – give it all to me because I deserve it

15) NO SECOND CHANCE TO MAKE A FIRST IMPRESSION

- Once I hate you, you are history

16) GET ALL THE LIARS IN THE SAME ROOM

- Let's gather everyone together so I can tell you how great I am

17) ALWAYS TELL THE TRUTH (DO NOT LIE, CHEAT OR STEAL)

- Unless it makes me look good

18) NEVER MAKE A CAREER DECISION BASED SOLELY ON YOUR PRESENT BOSS

- Because that would mean all of you would quit

19) VIEWS ON MANAGEMENT:

- Managers are here to make sure all of you think I am great

20) ELIMINATE ROADBLOCKS AND EXCUSES – PER-
   CEIVED OR REAL

   • There should be nothing standing in the way of you serv-
      ing me

21) WALK THE TALK

   • Remember, I am king and I control your destiny – make
      that apparent in your actions

22) HAVE FUN – or find a job or organization that can give it
   to you

   • You better have fun or I will continue firing people!

====

I.M. Boss would regularly tell us that our only job was to make him look good. In other words, we were there to serve *him*. With regularity, I would hear "This is MY house and we will do it *my* way!!!!" either booming from his office or being shouted in my face.

I chuckle when I think about the possibility of screaming at my wife in this way if I wanted her to iron every one of my shirts with light starch. She would tell me to "pound salt" pretty fast and that I was lucky she was even doing my laundry.

In one instance, Mary, our contract administrator and I.M. Boss's assistant, was working with one of our salespeople and our legal department on finalizing a contract with a large client–to–be. She received a call from I.M. Boss just before what was supposed to be the final conference call regarding this contract. I.M. Boss needed Mary to be available to make some travel reservations for him. When Mary told him she needed to get on this call to finalize this contract, I.M. Boss exploded, "I don't care about any contract, just wait by your phone so you can take care of me first!"

Is this how Jesus would have handled this situation? I don't think so.

Did Jesus send away the crowds when He wanted to spend some quality time with His disciples? He could have but instead He talked with them and He fed them.

Did Jesus ask for His disciples to wash His feet during His last supper? He could have. He certainly deserved at least that for all He had done for His disciples. He certainly deserved that for all the miracles and healings He had performed.

And ... He certainly deserved that for what He was about to do for the world.

But no, instead He washed His followers' feet. He made it very clear that He was there to serve.

> *It was just before the Passover Feast. Jesus knew that the time had come for him to leave this world and go to the Father. Having loved his own who were in the world, he now showed them the full extent of his love ... so he got up from the meal, took off his outer clothing, and wrapped a towel around his waist. After that he poured water into a basin and began to wash his disciples' feet, drying them with the towel that was wrapped around him.*
>
> (John 13:1, 4–5)

Let's think about that for a second. We are talking about the greatest leader to ever walk this earth. He didn't ask for a thing! Not even a pat on the back!

Not only was He the greatest *leader* that ever lived but also the greatest *servant* that ever lived. Perhaps that is *why* He was the greatest leader!

Yes, I know that many people have washed the feet of

others. Yes, I know people who have fed others. Yes, I know that many people have healed others. But I don't know of anyone, other than Christ, who gave his life for us so that we could have everlasting life. He doesn't even ask us to do anything other than to believe in Him (to learn more about this see Appendix A). He is the epitome of a servant leader!

One more example Jesus gave us of this servant attitude is incredible to me. In the gospel of John, after Jesus was crucified and resurrected, He appeared to the disciples while they were fishing. They were having difficulty catching fish so Jesus told them to throw the net to the other side of the boat and they immediately caught 153 fish.

I think most of us miss something very important here. Jesus then takes them to a place where He had started a fire. He was preparing some fish and bread for them to eat. Remember, this is the Lord, who just died a horrible death and then rose to fulfill the prophecies. Yet it was not beneath Him to fix breakfast for everyone there.

Webster's says that a servant is . . . *a person devoted to another or to a cause.* Okay, what does *devoted* really mean? Webster's defines devote as . . . *to give up (oneself or one's time, energy, . . .) to some purpose, activity, or person.*

According to this definition, serving is more than simply doing something for someone else. It is actually *giving* of ourselves, our time and/or our energy to someone else or to something else.

I think that is an understatement when it came to Jesus. Let's look at some of the things that Jesus gave up for us:

- His home with His mother and earthly father
- His friends at home
- His job as a carpenter

- His security
- A life without persecution and ridicule
- A life without pain and suffering
- His life!

What about other Biblical leaders? John the Baptist gave up his head. As we discussed earlier, Moses gave up his life as an Egyptian prince to live as a shepherd. After much convincing by God, he also left what he was doing to follow God's commands to lead. He even left his feelings of inadequacy!

Joseph gave up his freedom and was forced into slavery, then later wrongly accused of a crime and placed in jail. Even though these situations could have beaten him, Joseph chose to give of himself and to serve – regardless of his situation or his surroundings. Because of his serving nature, he was noticed by those in authority, which paid off for him in the end.

Paul gave up everything to preach the gospel to the Gentiles. In 2 Corinthians, Paul tells us some of what he went through to serve God:

> *"Five times I received from the Jews the forty lashes minus one. Three times I was beaten with rods, once I was stoned, three times I was shipwrecked, I spent a night and a day in the open sea, I have been constantly on the move. I have been in danger from rivers, in danger from bandits, in danger from my own countrymen, in danger from Gentiles; in danger in the city, in danger in the country, in danger at sea; and in danger from false brothers. I have labored and toiled and have often gone without sleep; I have known hunger and thirst and have often gone without food; I have been cold and naked."*
>
> (2 Corinthians 11:23–27)

Paul also tells us his purpose in Romans 15:17, *Therefore I glory in Christ Jesus in my service to God.* Paul was also a servant leader.

I received the following in an email recently, which gives another great example of servant leadership:

An article in National Geographic several years ago provided a penetrating picture of God's wings. After a forest fire in Yellowstone National Park, forest rangers began their trek up a mountain to assess the inferno's damage. One ranger found a bird literally petrified in ashes perched statuesquely on the ground at the base of a tree.

Somewhat sickened by the eerie sight, he knocked over the bird with a stick. When he gently struck it, three tiny chicks scurried from under their dead mother's wings. The loving mother, keenly aware of impending disaster, had carried her offspring to the base of the tree and had gathered them under her wings.

Instinctively knowing that the toxic smoke would rise, she could have flown to safety but had refused to abandon her babies. Then the blaze had arrived and the heat had scorched her small body – the mother remained steadfast.

Because she had been willing to die, those under the cover of her wings would live.

Sounds like Jesus doesn't it?

He will cover you with his feathers, and under his wings you will find refuge: his faithfulness will be your shield and rampart.

(Psalm 91:4)

Tom or Sue?

You work with Tom who is an extremely hard worker. He achieves more than anyone else in your department. Tom does nothing for anyone else, however. Before doing any task, he asks himself, "How will this help me?" If it benefits him, he will do the task with gusto.

Sue also works hard. She is also very helpful to everyone in your department and even those outside your area. Before doing a task, Sue asks herself, "Will this help make someone's life easier?" If the answer is yes, she will give it her all.

The decision is coming soon, on which one of these two will be your next boss. Who do you think will be the better leader? Based on servant–hood alone, clearly Sue would be the best choice.

Those we lead want to know that we are willing to work and that we are there to help them. I hope you had an opportunity to work for someone who had a *servant's heart*. If you have, do you remember how comforting it was for you?

---

*"And whoever wants to be first must be slave of all.
For even the Son of Man did not come to be served, but
to serve and to give His life as a ransom for many."*
(Mark 10:44–45)

*"For who is greater, the one who is at the table or the
one who serves? Is it not the one at the table? But I am
among you as one who serves."*
(Luke 22:27)

You, my brothers, were called to be free. But do not use your freedom to indulge the sinful nature, rather, serve one another in love.

(Galatians 5:13)

"For even the Son of Man did not come to be served but to serve, and to give his life as a ransom for many."

(Mark 10:45)

"I tell you the truth: Among those born of women there has not risen anyone greater than John the Baptist; yet he who is least in the kingdom of heaven is greater than he."

(Matthew 11:11)

Who, being in very nature God, did not consider equality with God something to be grasped, but made himself nothing, taking the very nature of a servant, being made in human likeness.

(Philippians 2:6–7)

CHAPTER 5
FORGIVING LEADERSHIP

"Failure is only an opportunity to more
intelligently begin again."
– Henry Ford

"Failure should be our teacher, not our undertaker.
Failure is delay, not defeat. It is a temporary detour, not
a dead end. Failure is something we can avoid only by
saying nothing, doing nothing, and being nothing."
– Denis Waitley

"Mistakes are painful when they happen, but years later
a collection of mistakes is what is called experience."
– Denis Waitley

"Forgiveness is not an emotion, it's a decision."
– Randall Worley

"If you wish to travel far and fast, travel light. Take off all
your envies, jealousies, unforgiveness, selfishness, and fears."
– Glenn Clark

"Never does the human soul appear so strong as when
it foregoes revenge, and dares forgive an injury."
– E. H. Chapin

There was once a couple that had been married for more than 60 years. They had shared everything. They had talked about everything. They had kept no secrets from each other, except that the little old woman had kept a shoebox in the top of her closet that she had cautioned her husband never to open nor ask her about.

Years went by and he had never given thought to the box in the closet. One day the little old woman got very sick and the doctor said she would not recover. In trying to sort out their affairs, the little old man took down the shoebox and took it to his wife's bedside. She agreed that it was time that he should know what was in the box.

When he opened it, he found two crocheted doilies and a stack of money totaling $25,000.

He asked her about the contents. "When we were to be married," she said, "my grandmother told me the secret to a happy marriage was to never argue. She told me that if I ever got angry with you, I should just keep quiet and crochet a doily."

The little old man was so moved; he had to fight back tears. Only two precious doilies were in the box. She had only been angry with him two times in all those years of living and loving. He almost burst with happiness. "Honey," he said, "that explains the doilies, but what about all of this money? Where did it come from?"

"Oh," she said, "that's the money I made from selling doilies."

<hr>

In our work environment, all of us who worked for I.M. Boss knew that if we ever got on I.M. Boss's "bad" side we were history. He once told another manager in the sales department, who reported to me in the spring of 2003, "Joe, when I leave this company, I am going to take you with me to wherever I land. You are really good." Joe had to be thinking, "What do you mean when you leave the company?" This was one committed leader wasn't it?

Not three months later, the tide had changed. Joe was on I.M. Boss's radar screen and I.M. Boss had an itchy trigger finger. Many times, he would tell me I needed to "kill" (fire) Joe. I.M. Boss would regularly tell his staff that Joe was worthless and we needed to get rid of him.

What happened in that three–month time span to make I.M. Boss do a complete 180 regarding Joe? I don't know *exactly* what happened, but somewhere along the way, Joe got on I.M. Boss's "bad" side.

It could have been that Joe did something to make I.M. Boss look bad. It could have been that something didn't go well and I.M. Boss assumed that Joe was at fault. It could have been that I.M. Boss had a bad dream about Joe. Who knows? It could have been that the phase of the moon was a contributing factor!

I.M. Boss twisted around the old adage and assumed that "you are guilty until proven innocent." He assumed that all employees are liars, cheaters and, in general, rotten people. After all, why else would they be in the low–life, working class?

Eventually, I.M. Boss made me fire Joe. It was the week before Christmas and Joe and his wife were expecting triplets in January. What a guy my boss was! In the end, I was able to work with Human Resources to allow Joe to resign and receive a fair severance package. Joe found work shortly thereafter and was employed in a much healthier environment.

Unfortunately, I saw this happen with numerous people

during the year and a half I was working with I.M. Boss. I even saw it more up close and personal than I wanted to as it happened to me.

At the beginning of the year, I.M. Boss proudly told corporate we would grow the company sales by 25% (while we had grown only 6% the year prior). He actually bragged to corporate that we would be the fastest growing division in the company. He made these claims and he really didn't have a clue about our business.

Toward the end of the year, we fell behind in achieving the goal. I.M. Boss felt that management needed to "beat" the sales force to spur them into action even though half of the group had been newly hired. (As mentioned earlier, it generally takes eighteen months for a good salesperson to get up to speed.) I.M. Boss said to me, "I don't think you understand the severity of this! I am not going to be the whipping boy for the sales force! People are concerned about my behavior and I am concerned about people's lack of credibility and lack of performance! Then we have our disaster with our new hires. You want to defend them? I can't defend *you* anymore if you want to defend them!!!"

I.M. Boss pulled me in his office and told me that our sales force was terrible. For example, he pointed out Cindy, who was struggling at the beginning of the year and needed to be fired. I explained that her results over the past six months show she is now our top salesperson. I.M. Boss said, "Jim, there you go defending people again! You are too close to these people! You are too nice to them! You need to yell at them if you want to be an effective leader! They don't respect you because you are too nice!"

The next day, I.M. Boss decided to look at those new hires who had been with us from one to six months. He figured out what we were paying them in salary and commission. The way he looked at it, they were not an investment that would pay off for us in a year and a half, rather they needed to pay off immediately. As I mentioned earlier, he had called all of the new reps into our office from around the country. He proceeded to tell them how awful they were. He wrote each of their salaries on the board for all to see and told them that they weren't going to make it since they have cost the company more money than they have made for the company. One of the salespeople there had only been with the company two weeks and I.M. Boss had already written him off! Sounds like a motivating meeting, doesn't it?

We had another sales rep named Ron whom I.M. Boss called "a top notch person and sales guy." That was until the fateful day that Ron was trying to do something pro–active to help secure more business from one of his clients. The day prior, I.M. Boss had said he wanted to be involved in all pricing discussions (apparently because he did not trust me anymore).

Ron had developed a pricing incentive to encourage one of his clients to do more business with us. I sent the proposal to I.M. Boss for his approval, per his instructions. He replied with a scathing email telling us that this was foolish. I.M. Boss then called a conference with me and Ron where he screamed at us and told us, "Get your &%$# together before you present something and waste my time on &*^% like this!!!! Why would we do something so &%#@ing stupid. Who is the &%#@ing idiot who put this together? Why should I do this?!!" Ron then agreed that he made a mistake. I.M. Boss kept going on and continued asking Ron what his problem was even after Ron admitted he made a mistake. I.M. Boss would not back down. "You've presented this to the customer, haven't you Ron!?"

Ron calmly responded that he had not presented anything to the customer. I.M. Boss then proceeded to call him a stupid person and worse. He again accused Ron of presenting this to the customer. Ron then said "I.M. Boss, I haven't presented &^%$ yet!"

I.M. Boss then responded, "I don't have time to deal with this. Don't you ever swear at me again Ron or you're out of here! This is my ship and you will do what I say! Don't ever propose something like this that is this stupid! We'll reconvene in twenty minutes!"

When we got back together twenty to thirty minutes later, I.M. Boss said he was going to help Ron now. However, he continued to hammer on Ron. I.M. Boss kept asking why he should want to lose money. He said, "Ron, you are golden. You are paid on revenue growth, but our shareholders lose money!"

Later, after conferring with our vice president of finance, I.M. Boss discovered that Ron's idea was a good one after all. The tirade was for naught! However, from that point on, I.M. Boss would tell people that Ron was stupid and should not be one of our employees.

GOD GIVES SECOND CHANCES

God gives second chances. It is incredible to me, as I read through Scripture, how God is so forgiving. One can read in the Bible how God was continually forgotten and ignored. I don't think I could be that forgiving if I were as forgotten as God was and still is.

I think God gives multiple chances for two main reasons:

First, He loves each and every one of us so much that He gave His only Son to die just to save us (John 3:16). That is love!

Second, God wants to model to us how we should live.

The Bible says we need to forgive each other – *Bear with each other and forgive whatever grievances you may have against one another. Forgive as the Lord forgave you.* (Colossians 3:13)

Throughout the Bible, God is very patient with humanity. Throughout Scripture, even in the midst of miracles that God was performing, the people continued to totally disregard His Word. They worshiped idols, they murdered, they raped. You get the picture. As a whole, they did not behave like nice Christians.

Is this any different than today? I don't think so. Many of us are living for our financial security, our next new BMW, our next vacation or the new hot tub for our back yard. The Bible says, *"For where your treasure is, there your heart will be also."* (Matthew 6:21) In other words, we are worshiping "idols." (Isn't there a commandment telling us not to do that?). We also continue to have murders. We continue to have rapes, etc.

In Biblical times, God was patient with the people just as He is now. He is not happy, but He still loves us. Have you ever heard of the phrase, "God hates the sin but loves the sinner?" Thank heavens for that!

Throughout the books of Kings and Chronicles, I am amazed that God did not just blow up the planet and start over! These people just didn't get it. Occasionally there were some kings and leaders who did and they pleased God, but the majority thumbed their noses at Him. God has unbelievable patience!

One of the greatest leaders in the Bible was Moses. Did you know that he was a murderer?

One day, after Moses had grown up, he went out to where his own people were and watched them at their hard labor. He saw an Egyptian beating a Hebrew, one

of his own people. Glancing this way and that and see-
ing no one, he killed the Egyptian and hid him in the
sand.

(Exodus 2:11, 12)

Could that be how you and I sometimes react to situations? No, we don't go out and kill people we don't like, but sometimes we treat them with contempt and we don't give them a chance. God is different. He not only does not condemn us, He actually looks for ways to use us for His benefit (and ours). He has compassion on us and that is hard for many of us to understand.

Sometime after Moses murdered a man, God actually chose Moses to be the leader of the Israelites; to lead them out of the bondage of Egypt. (Exodus 3:2–22) Does this mean that Moses pleased God in all ways from here on? No. When God was teaching Moses what to do, Moses said *"O Lord, please send someone else to do it."* Then the Lord's anger burned against Moses. . . (Exodus 4:13–14) But God did not yell or scream. He did not go crazy. He did not throw things or threaten Moses. What He did was to calmly instruct Moses and reassure him.

Now this doesn't mean that we, as leaders in our business are to let others walk all over us. However, we are instructed to give people *second chances* with compassion.

David was another great Biblical leader. He was a king with many wives – don't you wonder about their marriage practices? One day while out for a stroll around his compound, he saw a beautiful woman, named Bathsheba, bathing and sent for her.

His pride and lust got the better of him. Even though she was married to someone else, he slept with her and she became pregnant. To attempt to cover up his misdeed, he ordered Bathsheba's husband to the front lines to be killed in battle. He then took Bathsheba as his wife and she bore him a son.

As you could imagine, God was not pleased about this. God sent Nathan as a messenger to tell David that he had sinned and that God was not happy. Nathan said:

> *"There were two men in a certain town, one rich and the other poor. The rich man had a very large number of sheep and cattle, but the poor man had nothing except one little ewe lamb he had bought. He raised it, and it grew up with him and his children. It shared his food, drank from his cup and even slept in his arms. It was like a daughter to him.*

> *"Now a traveler came to the rich man, but the rich man refrained from taking one of his own sheep or cattle to prepare a meal for the traveler who had come to him. Instead, he took the ewe lamb that belonged to the poor man and prepared it for the one who had come to him."*

> *David burned with anger against the man and said to Nathan, "As surely as the Lord lives, the man who did this deserves to die! He must pay for that lamb four times over, because he did such a thing and had no pity."*

> *Then Nathan said to David, "You are the man! This is what the Lord, the God of Israel, says: 'I anointed you king over Israel, and I delivered you from the hand of Saul. I gave your master's house to you, and your master's wives into your arms. I gave you the house of Israel and Judah. And if all this had been too little, I would have given you even more. Why did you despise the word of the Lord by doing what is evil in his eyes?*

You struck down Uriah the Hittite with the sword and took his wife to be your own. You killed him with the sword of the Ammonites. Now, therefore, the sword will never depart from your house, because you despised me and took the wife of Uriah to be your own.'"

(2 Samuel 12:1–12)

Realizing his terrible mistake, David said, *"I have sinned against the Lord." Nathan replied, "The Lord has taken away your sin. You are not going to die. But because by doing this you have made the enemies of the Lord show utter contempt, the son born to you will die."* (2 Samuel 12:13, 14) Soon thereafter, the baby became ill and died.

Later Bathsheba and David had another son named Solomon who became a great Biblical leader in his own right. God even refers to David in Acts 13:22 as " . . . *a man after my own heart."* This shows first, God's never–ending compassion and forgiveness for us. Second, it shows that while God forgives us, we cannot escape the consequences of our actions.

This speaks volumes to us as leaders. There needs to be consequences for actions; however, those consequences must be doled out with love and compassion. It also tells us that we, as leaders in our homes and in our businesses, must forgive mistakes and not continue to bring them up.

This shows me that God is the eternal optimist. That is how we need to be as leaders. We should not assume the worst about people. That could lead to the delusion that everyone is "out to get us," which happened with my boss. People will want to follow us when they know that we can see the good in them. Proverbs 25:21 tells us, *If your enemy is hungry, give him food to eat; if he is thirsty, give him water to drink . . .* Even if someone wrongs us or makes a mistake, we need to act with kindness and compassion toward them.

Think of the nastiest people you can. Think again of even nastier people than that. Okay, do you have them pictured in your mind? What would you like God to do to them? Don't you wish that God would exercise His judgment on them?

If you were like me you certainly wouldn't want to be near them in any way. You might profess that you listen to God and He directs your life, but what if God spoke to you and instructed you to go share the gospel with this group of people. Would you want to run? I know I would!

That is exactly what happened to Jonah. He was told by God to go to Nineveh, a very corrupt city, to preach the gospel. He refused. In fact, he took a ship in the opposite direction to get as far away from Nineveh as possible. We know what happened next. A storm came up and Jonah volunteered to be thrown overboard because he knew that his disobedience was the cause of the storm. He went into the sea and immediately the storm was calmed.

Then he was swallowed by a whale – *The Lord provided a great fish to swallow Jonah.* (Jonah 1:17) Notice the word "provided." It doesn't say the Lord "*punished* Jonah by sending a great fish" rather it says that God is saving Jonah – He is actually giving him a second chance by making him a human snack.

When our children, or the people who work for us, defy our authority, how does that make us feel? I don't know about you, but I get pretty frustrated and steamed. But not God – what amazing compassion! After Jonah prayed for forgiveness, God commanded the great fish to vomit Jonah up onto dry land. Then God told Jonah a second time to go to Nineveh to deliver His message. I think even *I* might listen at that point!

Jonah did go to Nineveh and told the people that unless they repent, God would destroy the city. The people of Nineveh were remarkably receptive. They said, "Wow, we didn't know that is how we are supposed to behave!" They listened and repented.

There is another part of the *second chance* in the book of Jonah. Why did God want Jonah to go to Nineveh? Wasn't that city full of wicked and evil people? *The word of the Lord came to Jonah son of Amittai: "Go to the great city of Nineveh and preach against it, because its wickedness has come up before me."* Did you catch that last part? *"Its wickedness has come up before me."* When wickedness comes up before most of us, we hope that God will take care of it for us. We want them to pay. God has a different view—one of great love, patience and forgiveness.

In fact, Jonah, after doing what God had asked, became very dismayed that God was so compassionate with these horrible people. He thought they should receive the full wrath of God. So he went out on a hill overlooking the great city to see what God would do. God actually *provided a vine* to grow to shade Jonah where he sat (again, what compassion!). Jonah was very grateful.

However, the next day God *provided a worm* that chewed on the vine and killed it. Jonah was very distraught. God then said, *"You have been very concerned about this vine, though you did not tend it or make it grow. It sprang up overnight. But Nineveh has more than 120,000 people who cannot tell their right hand from their left, and many cattle as well. Should I not be concerned about that great city?"* (Jonah 4:10–11)

It's as if God is saying, "Hey, chill out Jonah. Why are you complaining about that vine when you had nothing to do with its growth? It came and went in one day so you should just be glad that it was here for you that one day. I created Nineveh, it has been around a long time, and it is full of many people. The fact is that they *don't know what they don't know*. All they need is for someone to tell them the truth. I want to give them that chance." How incredible is that?

Haven't each of us done some things of which we were grateful for a second chance? How many second chances have you had? How many second chances have you given?

In what I think is the greatest example of giving us a second chance, Revelation tells us of Jesus' coming back to rapture His church. All of His followers will be taken with Him to heaven. Everyone else will be left behind. But that is not the end of it.

God will then rain down judgments and plagues on the Earth. This will continue for seven years. The first three and a half years is known as The Tribulation and is supposed to be a terrible time. The last three and a half years is known as The Great Tribulation as it will make the first three and a half years seem like a cakewalk. Terrible things will happen, plagues will be placed on people, locusts will invade the earth, all water on the planet will turn to blood, and more.

God's purpose is to get the attention of those who are left on the Earth. He wants them to finally "get it;" to accept Jesus as their Savior. If they do, they will be saved when Jesus comes a second time, after the seven year Tribulation. If they don't, they are doomed for eternity.

Think about that. That is awesome to me. God has spent His time, since Adam and Eve were in the garden until the end of time as we know it, watching His people turn their backs on Him. What does He do? He takes His followers to live with Him and He still gives everyone else another chance. He doesn't just give everyone one minute – He doesn't just give an hour – He doesn't give just a week or a month – He gives seven years! What incredible love!

God also gives us a great example of the forgiveness of others in the story of Joseph, which we discussed earlier. In Genesis, we learn of Joseph who was one of Jacob's twelve sons. He was clearly Jacob's favorite. Jacob made Joseph's brothers do all the work while Joseph hung out at home, enjoying his privileged life.

Jacob then gave Joseph a specially woven coat of many colors that would be fit for royalty. This made Joseph's brothers even more jealous of him. Then Joseph, not knowing when to keep his mouth shut, piled on even more by revealing a dream he had where he would rule over all of his brothers.

Needless to say, they were furious, so they plotted to kill him. Rather than killing Joseph, one of the brothers persuaded the others to sell him into slavery instead. They did this and told Jacob, their father, that Joseph had been killed.

Through this, Joseph rode the roller coaster of emotions. He found favor with his master and was placed in charge of his house. There he was falsely accused of raping his master's wife and he was thrown in prison. He remained in jail for several years and probably wondered if he would ever find freedom.

Finally, he was released from jail. Because of his leadership ability and his ability to interpret dreams, Pharaoh placed him in charge of Egypt. Sometime later, a famine hit the land (which Joseph had accurately predicted) and people from all over came to Egypt for food (where Joseph had the foresight to store food to prepare for the famine).

Jacob, who learned of the food in Egypt, sent his sons to purchase food for the household. His sons made the journey to Egypt to buy grain not suspecting who they will run into.

They came to Joseph, who had the perfect opportunity for a wonderful payback. He could have thrown them in jail, had them tortured or even killed. Whatever he wanted to do with them, he could have done.

What did he do? He *forgave* them! I have a hard time comprehending that sometimes. He had the perfect opportunity to say, "I get the last laugh! The joke's on you! Paybacks are tough!" He doesn't. He actually thanked them! That's right; in Genesis 45:5 Joseph told them not to feel bad about what they had done, because it was done for a greater good, God's work.

Put yourself in Joseph's brothers' shoes. While they were thrilled to see that Joseph was alive and well, I am sure they were worried about what their father, Jacob would do to them when he found out the true story of what they had done to Joseph. Well, Joseph sensed this and did something incredible – he told them what to say to Jacob (Genesis 45:9–13).

If Joseph can do that for the unthinkable wrong that was done to him, shouldn't we forgive those who hurt us?

Consider this. Did you know that history books are full of stories of gifted people who were overlooked by others until someone believed in them and gave them a second chance; or a third, or a fourth? Isaac Newton did poorly in grade school. Hayden gave up on Beethoven as he felt Beethoven seemed slow and had no musical talent. Werner Von Braun failed ninth–grade algebra. Michael Jordan was cut from his high school basketball team. A newspaper editor fired Walt Disney because he lacked good ideas. Albert Einstein first spoke when he was four years old and could not read until he was seven.

Sylvester Stallone was rejected time after time before someone agreed to produce *Rocky*. Just think, if someone didn't give Stallone that second chance, or that third chance, our grand-children wouldn't have the opportunity to see *Rocky XXV*!

JACK OR CARL?

Jack and Carl are both up for promotions to be your manager. While Jack is an easy–going guy and he works very hard, he seems to not have forgiven you when you took his favorite parking place on that rainy day last year. In fact, he brings it up quite a bit. You also notice that he tends to hold grudges with other co–workers as he is often talking about how he has been wronged.

Carl is also easy going and works hard. Last month, you accidentally tripped on the way back from the coffee machine and spilled coffee all over Carl's new pants. You told him you were sorry and that you would pay for any dry–cleaning cost but Carl simply chuckled and said, "It was great running into you." Carl has not mentioned a word of this to anyone since.

Whom would you rather have running your department? I believe that Carl would be the hands–down winner with all other things being equal. A leader who *forgives* can inspire people.

Romans 8:28 says, *And we know that in all things God works for the good of those who love him, who have been called according to his purpose.* Knowing that, why do we need to worry about something someone did and not forgive them? This verse tells us that God is going to work it all out for good in the end anyway. This doesn't mean that we shouldn't use this as a learning tool, but this shows us that there is no reason not to forgive.

Bear with each other and forgive whatever grievances you may have against one another. Forgive as the Lord forgave you.

Colossians 3:13

"For if you forgive men when they sin against you, your heavenly Father will also forgive you. But if you do not forgive men their sins, your Father will not forgive your sins."

Matthew 6:14–15

"And when you stand praying, if you hold anything against anyone, forgive him, so that your Father in heaven may forgive you your sins."

Mark 11:25

"Do not judge, and you will not be judged. Do not condemn, and you will not be condemned. Forgive, and you will be forgiven."

Luke 6:37

"If you forgive anyone his sins, they are forgiven; if you do not forgive them, they are not forgiven."

John 20:23

'This is what you are to say to Joseph: I ask you to forgive your brothers the sins and the wrongs they committed in treating you so badly.' Now please forgive the sins of the servants of the God of your father." When their message came to him, Joseph wept.

Genesis 50:17

CHAPTER 6
LISTENING LEADERSHIP

"Listening builds trust, the
foundation of all lasting relationships."
– Brian Tracy

"It seems rather incongruous that in a
society of super sophisticated communication, we
often suffer from a shortage of listeners."
– Erma Bombeck

"Seek first to understand, then to be understood."
– Stephen Covey

"One of the greatest gifts you can give to
anyone is the gift of attention."
– Jim Rohn

A couple of rednecks are out in the woods hunting when one of them falls to the ground. He doesn't seem to be breathing and his eyes are rolled back in his head.

The other guy whips out his cell phone and calls 911.

He frantically tells the operator, "Bubba is dead! What can I do?"

The operator, in a calm, soothing voice says, "Just take it easy. I can help. First, let's make sure he's dead."

There is silence, and then a shot is heard.

The guy's voice comes back on the line and says, "Okay, now what?"

As this story about the rednecks illustrates – we can *hear* what is said without really *listening* to what is being communicated. The hunter above heard what the operator told him and technically did make sure that his hunting companion was dead. But had he really been listening, I don't think he would have shot his partner.

Listening is a skill that is sadly lacking, not only in the business offices of our country, but at all levels of society. Did you ever wonder why there are speech classes in schools but no *listening* classes?

As mentioned earlier, it is said, "people don't care how much you know until they know how much you care." One of the best ways to show how much you care is simply to *listen.*

Unfortunately, that is not what I.M. Boss, the leader of our company did. He always seemed to have preconceived ideas, which wouldn't allow him to hear what someone would say. He acted like he had two mouths and only one ear.

Instead of actively listening, it was as if he were always thinking of what to say so that he could come off as "brilliant" or "sharp." After looking back on my time working with him, this does not surprise me because, as I mentioned earlier, his primary goal (and unfortunately ours) was to make him look good.

This has been something I have struggled with throughout my life. Occasionally I will catch myself thinking about my response before the person I am supposed to be listening to is finished. By the way, this is not listening. I now try to tell myself that if what I have to say is important enough, the thought will still be there when I have finished listening. I still have a long way to go, but this does work.

In one instance, I.M. Boss had an issue with a $10 million liability limit that a client wanted in their contract. This was a new development in the negotiations and they were simply discussing it. This was going to be one of our company's largest accounts and our salesperson had worked for over two years on it. The following is how it went between I.M. Boss and Lou, our salesperson:

"Lou, will the client reject this if we only offer them a $5 million liability limit?"

Lou, "I don't know."

In a very condescending tone, "Lou, I'm very busy so we'll try again. When I ask you a question, let's try to answer it. Do you know?"

Lou said, "I believe they will reject."

"So you don't know. How long have you been working with them? And you still don't know?"

Lou tried to respond to let him know that this was a new development with a new person from their company but I.M.

Boss cut him off, "I got it Lou, you don't know. I don't want to hear anymore!"

Brilliant example of listening, don't you think?

Later, when discussing this same account (that was successfully negotiated), I.M. Boss was upset that he was not involved earlier in the negotiations (even though he never wanted to be involved in early stages as it was beneath him). He blamed the sales rep even though the rep followed current procedures.

He said to me, "Well, Lou obviously didn't do a very good job."

I said, "I.M. Boss, he did the best he could and in the end he landed the account!"

I.M. Boss replied, "Now you are in defense mode again. We need to get out of this 'Never–Never Land' and face the facts. We have been made to look like a fool in my house – so I look like a fool. Lou didn't do this properly!"

Again, he had preconceived ideas and was not open to listening to facts.

Another example was during a conference call with I.M. Boss, the vice president of finance and another salesperson named Roger regarding another huge client. Roger presented updated pricing to I.M. Boss showing him that our margin was within the boundaries that I.M. Boss and Finance had approved.

During the call, I.M. Boss said he didn't agree with Roger's margin figures even though our vice president of finance did. He rejected the pricing and was not open to discussing it any further.

I asked, "Can I ask a question?"

I.M. Boss totally shut me out by saying, "Only if your

question has nothing to do with pricing or margin on this account."

I.M. Boss then asked Roger about the applications involved and Roger responded, "That is a good question, it is a mad mix of applications."

I.M. Boss said in a condescending tone, "Roger, I want you to try something new and just answer my questions. Let's leave the narratives out and just answer my questions!"

Later in the discussion, I.M. Boss said, "What is your strategy!!?"

I told I.M. Boss that our strategy was to get phase one and two up and running as that is what the client wanted (in fact that is the only way the client would do business with us). Then we were going to discuss the next phases with them as to how we would proceed.

He said, "I don't see a strategy!!! I'm done! I'm done! We don't have a strategy!"

BIBLICAL LISTENING

The Bible is full of examples of God's people listening to and some *not* listening to God. It also has some examples of God listening to His people.

God speaks to us in many ways: through the Bible, through circumstances in our lives, through other people and through that still small voice in our head (the Holy Spirit). We are instructed in Scripture to continually seek God's truth; to listen to Him. Psalm 46:10 begins with these words of advice, *"Be still, and know that I am God."* In other words, "Settle down, relax and listen to Me, for I am God."

Most of us have heard of Noah. We are told that Noah

was a good man, *"Noah was a righteous man, blameless among the people of his time, and he walked with God."* (Exodus 6:9) God did not think so highly of the rest of the people who had become very evil. God decided to flood the earth and start over. Because of his high standing in the eyes of God, God decided to spare Noah and allow him to build an ark that would save Noah and his family as well as the animal kingdom.

God spoke to Noah and instructed him to begin building a large ark that was the length of one and a half football fields and as high as a four–story building. Noah began immediately. He did not question why he was building a ship so far from water. He did not question why the boat needed to be so big. He did not question why he was going to spend years of his life building this large watercraft (it ended up taking him between 80 and 120 years!) He simply listened and obeyed.

Can you imagine the ridicule Noah had to hear from his friends and the people in his town? "Hey Noah, nice boat – too bad you can't get it to water!" Or, "Noah you've really lost it – you're nuts!" It had to take tremendous faith and courage to stand firm during those times. I am sure it helped knowing that he was following God's orders, but just the same, it had to be terribly difficult.

Just think what would have happened had Noah *not listened.*

Most of the great leaders of the Bible listened and obeyed. Moses listened to God tell and show him how Moses could do what he thought was impossible. Joseph listened to God and served with a cheerful heart even though he was placed in several terrible circumstances. Because they listened, they became some of the greatest leaders throughout history.

God also listens to us. Philippians 4:6–7 tells us, *Do not be anxious about anything, but in everything, by prayer and petition, with thanksgiving, present your requests to God. And the peace of God which transcends all understanding, will guard your hearts and minds in Christ Jesus.* What a wonderful promise!

Let's look more closely at that. God says that we should take *everything* to Him in prayer. He doesn't say, "I am really busy up here, so only bring the really critical stuff to Me." He says bring it *all* to Him, even if you lost your keys and you need His help to find them.

He says He will listen! Verse 7 tells us that we will have a peace that *will guard our hearts and minds.* That sounds pretty awesome, doesn't it? In order for this to happen, God needs to listen to us. Imagine that, God, the All Powerful, Creator of life and Protector of the universe *will listen* to you and me. Amazing! The only thing God asks is that we ask Him with thanksgiving in our hearts. Sounds like a fair request to me.

Well, we have established that God listens to us. It stands to reason that if God listens to *everything* we say to Him, even without an appointment, we should be listening to those we lead as well. But what if someone we are leading asks us to do something that is very contrary to our thinking?

A great example of this is found in Scripture:

Then the Lord said to Moses, "Go down, because your people, whom you brought up out of Egypt, have become corrupt. They have been quick to turn away from what I commanded them and have made themselves an idol cast in the shape of a calf. They have bowed down to it and sacrificed to it and have said, 'These are your gods, O Israel, who brought you out of Egypt.'

"I have seen these people," the Lord said to Moses, "and they are a stiff–necked people. Now leave me alone so that my anger may burn against them and that I may destroy them. Then I will make you into a great nation."

But Moses sought the favor of the Lord his God. "O Lord," he said, "why should your anger burn against your people, whom you brought out of Egypt with great power and a mighty hand? Why should the Egyptians say, 'It was with evil intent that he brought them out, to kill them in the mountains and to wipe them off the face of the earth'? Turn from your fierce anger; relent and do not bring disaster on your people. Remember your servants Abraham, Isaac and Israel, to whom you swore by your own self: 'I will make your descendants as numerous as the stars in the sky and I will give your descendants all this land I promised them, and it will be their inheritance forever.'" Then the Lord relented and did not bring on his people the disaster he had threatened.

(Exodus 32:7–14)

God said He was going to destroy the very people Moses was leading because He was so angry with them. Moses gave a good argument to the Lord so He decided to spare them. We don't see God do this often so why would God do this for Moses?

I believe the reason is that God wanted to show us as leaders that we need to put away our pride and listen to those we lead. They might just have a better idea. That doesn't mean we always have to do what they say, but if we *listen,* those we lead will be much more willing to *follow,* even if we don't do what they want.

God has promised that He will listen to us (Philippians 4:6–7). Don't you think this is the least we can do to those who follow us?

CHERYL OR STACEY?

Cheryl and Stacey are both up for a promotion to be your new manager.

Cheryl is a friendly person who works very hard. She works so hard that she doesn't seem to have time for any conversation, even if it is work related. When you talk with her, you notice that she looks at her watch often, is fidgety and finishes your sentences to make the conversation move along faster. While you respect her work ethic, Cheryl leaves you feeling less than important.

Stacey on the other hand, is also a hard worker but she can be found participating at times in conversation with other employees around the water cooler. Sometimes you overhear her having a conversation about work and sometimes you hear her discussing personal matters. Every time you speak with Stacey, she listens intently. You feel that to Stacey, you and what you say are very important. While she is involved in many conversations, Stacey never falls behind in her work.

Who would you like to be the next leader of your department? Though Stacey does not appear to work as hard as Cheryl, she clearly has better listening skills. A leader who is a listener can win any battle with his or her troops. Because they know their leader cares about them they will be willing to go the extra mile.

How do you feel when the person you are talking to is looking around the room, looking at his or her watch or obviously thinking about something else? How do you feel when you are listened to? If asked, how would those we lead feel about us when talking with us? Do they feel listened to? Let's listen to those we lead.

---

*God listened to Leah, and she became pregnant and bore
Jacob a fifth son.*

Genesis 30:17

*The priests and the Levites stood to bless the people, and
God heard them, for their prayer reached heaven, his
holy dwelling place.*

2 Chronicles 30:27

*Moses and Aaron were among his priests, Samuel was
among those who called on his name; they called on the
Lord and he answered them.*

Psalm 99:6

*The Lord has heard my cry for mercy; the Lord accepts
my prayer.*

Psalm 6:9

*So the people grumbled against Moses, saying, "What
are we to drink?" Then Moses cried out to the Lord, and
the Lord showed him a piece of wood. He threw it into
the water, and the water became sweet.*

Exodus 15:24–25

*Then Moses cried out to the Lord, "What am I to do with
these people? They are almost ready to stone me." The
Lord answered Moses. . .*

Exodus 17:4–5

*My dear brothers, take note of this: Everyone should be
quick to listen, slow to speak and slow to become angry.*

James 1:19

I call on the Lord in my distress, and he answers me.

Psalm 120:1

CHAPTER 7
INCLUSIVE LEADERSHIP

"A team is a group of people who may not be equal in
experience, talent or education but in commitment."
– Patricia Fripp

"Cooperation is working together agreeably . . .
Collaboration is working together aggressively; and
there's a world of difference between those two."
– John Maxwell

"Alone we can do so little; together we can do so much."
– Helen Keller

"Good leaders make people feel that they're at the
very heart of things, not at the periphery.
Everyone feels that he or she makes a difference to the
success of an organization. When that happens people
feel centered and that gives their work meaning."
– Warren Bennis

"You don't get the breaks unless you play
with the team instead of against it."
– Lou Gehrig

Three men are out in a boat when they hit a large rock and the boat sinks. They float ashore on a deserted island where they spend the next six months. One day one of the men finds a rusted old lamp washed up on the shore. He begins to polish it and a "Genie" pops out.

The Genie says, "Thank you for releasing me. You may have three wishes, but since there are three of you, each of you gets one wish."

The first man says, "Oh fantastic, please send me back home and let me resume my life where I left off."

Poof! He is gone.

The second says, "I miss my wife and kids so much. Please send me back to them."

Poof! He, too is gone.

The third one says, "I am feeling kind of alone and left out without my buddies here. Can you bring them back?"

━━━━━━━━━━━━━━━━━━━━━

When we looked at I.M. Boss's "22 Rules" (shown in chapter 4) and really boiled them down to their core meaning, we felt that I.M. Boss was saying, "You must worship me – I am the reason for your existence – I have all the power." Sadly, I think he truly believed this.

I.M. Boss so wanted everyone to know of his power, that he would do everything he could to stir the pot. He wanted to divide us, especially when things were not going well. I think this was done in order to take the negative focus off him.

He would regularly tell people in our office that someone

would be fired in a couple of weeks to show that he knew all and, " . . . you better watch out or you could be next." He would then add, " . . . you can't tell anyone or I will have to fire you also." This poor person would not only be intimidated, but now they would have to face their peer(s), and sometimes friend(s) knowing that they would not be with us in a couple of weeks. This was not only unfair to the employee being fired but it was terribly unfair to the one who I.M. Boss confided in, as they had to carry that burden with them.

After the meeting I discussed earlier where I.M. Boss put everyone's compensation package on the board for all to see, our sales force was feeling very divided. Our top salesperson earned the lowest salary! Though he earned the most commission, he was feeling very unappreciated and a little embarrassed.

We also had other new hires who saw that they were hired in at lower base salaries than their peers. Obviously, this did not promote a feeling of oneness, as a team should feel.

In another instance, I.M. Boss called our vice president of operations and me into his office to discuss a price increase we had put into effect. I was in charge of figuring out which clients were to receive the increase and our vice president of finance, Stacey was in charge of applying the increase.

Stacey had not had the time to apply the increase in the current month so I.M. Boss was not happy. He told me, "Jim, the fact that we did not get the increase is not your fault. It is Stacey's. But she is telling corporate that it is *your* fault. You need to watch your back because she is out to get you. Assume that when you talk with her that Carl (our corporate CFO) is sitting next to you. Stacey is a shark. Jimmy, watch your back, that is all I'm telling you."

Later, when I talked with Stacey about this, she told me that she had told corporate no such thing. In fact, *she* took the blame. She also added that I.M. Boss had told her that *I* was a shark and that *I* was telling stories about *her* to corporate. What a great way to build a cohesive team!

In many staff meetings and company–wide meetings, I.M. Boss would let everyone know that our corporate headquarters was not good at all – in fact they stunk! He would go out of his way to do this so that he would look better in our eyes. In reality, all this really did was put a wedge between our corporate office and our division and create an "us versus them" mentality.

It seemed that in all circumstances, whether it was preparing for a presentation to corporate, or talking about members of the corporate leadership team, all I.M. Boss wanted to do was " ... jam it down their throat." Remember, his only goal was to look good, and tearing others down, in his eyes, would help him to shine.

In addition to this, he would regularly criticize employees in front of their peers. So if Joe was criticized in front of his co–workers on the shop floor, he would probably feel very unimportant and down about his work. So when Joe would come to work, he would not only feel bad, but also he might get an attitude from others who worked with him.

JESUS AND INCLUSION

Could you imagine walking out your door and going into an office building and asking a busy executive to drop everything he is doing to follow you? How about going to a construction site and grabbing a foreman and telling him to leave the job site to follow you? Imagine going to the site of a home fire and talking with the insurance adjuster and convincing him to drop all he has going on and asking him to follow you. What about an IRS agent?

That seems like an impossible task. Simply asking others to leave their jobs seems very unlikely, but add to that the fact that each of these people would have other things going on in their lives. Maybe they are married. Maybe they have kids. Maybe they have bills to pay. Maybe they have church commitments. In any event, chances are very good they would have lots of other stuff going on.

You would be asking these people to not only give up their jobs, but also all of their other commitments. They probably won't see their friends much, if at all. They must leave it all behind.

Let's assume that you can "sell" them all on coming with you. What then? They are all so different. They look at each other and probably ask themselves, "Why is he in this elite group? In fact, why am I?" The IRS agent would probably get the funniest looks. How could you get them all focused on the same, seemingly impossible task?

What do you think now? Could you do it? Jesus did.

He not only convinced twelve people to give up everything and follow Him, He took them from different walks of life and formed a cohesive unit—a team—a family.

We don't know all of the occupations of Jesus' disciples but we do know that there were some fishermen and a lowly tax collector. There were some who were good speakers and leaders, and others who were shy and afraid. Some were greedy; some were impulsive; and some were ambitious. There were some who were leaders and others who were followers. There was one who was the best–known doubter of all time ("doubting" Thomas). There were some who would prove to be loyal and one who would betray Him.

Despite all of these differences, Jesus rallied the troops. He made them *one* team with *one* goal in mind.

But how did He do this?

I think many of the reasons are discussed in other areas of this book. When one becomes a leader with humility; a leader with compassion; a leader who is a servant; a leader who forgives; a leader who listens; a leader with integrity and a leader who is calm under pressure, an amazing thing happens. He or she has followers who are focused on the goal and focused on the good of the team. That is what Jesus did.

Another thing that Jesus did was that He typically corrected people in private. In Matthew, chapter 15 we see that Jesus walked on the water out to the boat the disciples were in. They were frightened and amazed. Peter, asked for permission to walk on the water also:

> *"Lord, if it's you," Peter replied, "tell me to come to you on the water."*
>
> *"Come," he said.*
>
> *Then Peter got down out of the boat, walked on the water and came toward Jesus. But when he saw the wind, he was afraid and, beginning to sink, cried out, "Lord save me!"*
>
> *Immediately, Jesus reached out his hand and caught him. "You of little faith," he said, "why did you doubt?"*
> (Matthew 14:28–31)

Notice that Jesus did not wait until they were back in the boat with the others to correct him. He did it right then, *while they were by themselves.*

You see, Peter actually showed a tremendous amount of faith to at least give it a shot. More so than the eleven others who remained dry. He just hadn't shown total faith and Jesus wanted to be sure to let him know that. Jesus didn't want to break Peter's spirit. I think chastising him in front of the group could have done that.

He built this group into a unit through powerful, yet humble teaching. He did not divide them because He did not let His ego get in the way. He had one goal and He did not want any egos to get in the way.

Why do some leaders divide while others pull teams together? I think in one word it is "humility." I find that the leaders who are humble do not have egos that pit different factions against each other for their own purposes. They recognize that the goal is greater than themselves. They don't want the credit, because they know to whom the credit really goes – to God.

Jesus wanted His team to be great. He knew that He was on this earth for one reason and one reason only – to glorify God. He did not let His own ego get in the way of this. He brought the disciples together even though it would have been very easy to divide them. Jesus was the epitome of a "team player." He was obviously not in this for Himself.

He didn't need any glory – it was all for God.

RALPH OR BETTY?

Ralph and Betty are both co–workers of yours. They are the finalists to fill the position as leader of your department.

Ralph is a diligent worker who always gets things done. He gets along well with everyone. He has a knack for including others in his successes and taking personal responsibility when things go badly. You have always marveled at this and thought of him as very secure. "Anyone who can act this way when promotions are on the line must be pretty special," you think to yourself.

Betty is also a hard worker. She also lets everyone know

it. Although she is fairly well liked, she rarely wants to be on teams, as she wants to show everyone how much she can do on her own. In addition, when others get attention, such as Ralph, she has been known to gossip about them to try to get public opinion against them. She reasons that this will help her in her career; "it's a 'dog–eat–dog' world, you know." She is proud of her accomplishments.

Would you like to see Ralph or Betty as your next boss? If it were based solely on his or her ability to build a team and include everyone, the clear choice would be Ralph.

When someone feels they are part of a team, they can accomplish much more than by themselves. This story I received in an email is a good illustration of that:

> *A man was lost while driving through the country. As he tried to read a map, he accidentally drove off the road into a ditch. Though he wasn't injured, his car was stuck deep in the mud. So the man walked to a nearby farm to ask for help.*
>
> *"Warwick can get you out of that ditch," said the farmer, pointing to an old mule standing in a field. The man looked at the haggardly mule and looked at the farmer who just stood there repeating, "Yep, old Warwick can do the job." The man figured he had nothing to lose. The two men and Warwick made their way back to the ditch.*
>
> *The farmer hitched the mule to the car. With a snap of the reigns he shouted, "Pull, Fred! Pull, Jack! Pull, Ted! Pull, Warwick!" And the mule pulled the car from the ditch with very little effort.*
>
> *The man was amazed. He thanked the farmer, patted*

the mule and asked, "Why did you call out all those other names before you called Warwick?"

The farmer grinned and said, "Old Warwick is just about blind. As long as he believes he is part of a team, he doesn't mind pulling."

Jesus knew their thoughts and said to them, "Every kingdom divided against itself will be ruined, and every city or household divided against itself will not stand."

Matthew 12:25

"If a kingdom is divided against itself, that kingdom cannot stand. If a house is divided against itself, that house cannot stand. And if Satan opposes himself and is divided, he cannot stand; his end has come."

Mark 3:24–26

Jesus knew their thoughts and said to them: "Any kingdom divided against itself will be ruined, and a house divided against itself will fall.

Luke 11:17

These are the men who divide you, who follow mere natural instincts and do not have the Spirit.

Jude 1:19

CHAPTER 8

LEADERSHIP WITH INTEGRITY

"I hope I shall always possess firmness and
virtue enough to maintain what I consider the most
enviable of all titles, the character of an honest man."
– George Washington

"Character is what you are in the dark."
– Dwight Moody

"If you want to take the meaning of the word integrity
and reduce it to its simplest terms, you'd conclude that a
man of integrity is a promise keeper. When he gives his
word, you can take it to the bank. His word is good."
– Bill McCartney

"The best index to a person's character is (a) how
he treats people who can't do him any good, and (b)
how he treats people who can't fight back."
– Abigail Van Buren

The hall of fame is only good as long as time shall be,

But keep in mind God's hall of fame is for eternity.

To have your name inscribed up there is greater by far,

Than all the praise and all the fame of any manmade star.

~ Author Unknown

"Quick Jim, what color are Barb's eyes?" I.M. Boss asked me one day. Barb was an employee who was cute and was rather well endowed. I.M. Boss thought this was hilarious when I could not tell him the color of her eyes. Little did he realize that I am not very observant when it comes to eye–color. He figured that I was mesmerized, as *he* was by her other "assets."

About another employee, he would ask me, "What do you think Beth would be like in bed?" Or he would say something like, "You did good in hiring Sally – she is a hottie!" Another favorite was, "Man, are we loaded with good looking women here!" This would be hours after telling us, "I love my wife! I am so lucky to have such an angel like her in my life. I love my wife!"

I.M. Boss even went so far as to try to keep an employee simply because she was cute. One of our female sales people, named Beth, gave me her two–weeks notice and I politely thanked her for her service and worked out a transition plan with her. She was very thankful and was eager to help out any way she could.

Several days later, I.M. Boss, called me into his office and said, "Jim, would you like to keep Beth?"

I said, "No, I think it is best she is moving on. Her performance has been a little down and she is tired of the travel. She and I have discussed this over the past several months and we think this is the best for her and for the company."

I.M. Boss replied, "Okay, but if you want to keep her we could offer her more money or do whatever." I thanked him but told him I did not want to do that as I thought she would be better off in another position elsewhere.

Approximately one week later, Beth called me to say she had had a change of heart and she would really like to stay. I asked what changed her mind and she told me that I.M. Boss had met with her the day before and told her she was doing great and that he really wanted her to stay.

Although I did not want to listen, I.M. Boss would talk to me frequently about what he would like Beth to do to him in bed. I think he wanted to be able to fantasize about this more, so the last thing he wanted was for her to leave!

This type of leader is very selfish. He is not willing to set the bar for everyone else. I.M. Boss had his "22 Rules." But in a way he was saying, "Here are your rules but I don't need to follow them, because I am the king."

Some of I.M. Boss's "22 Rules" we discussed earlier, happen to be good. One of them was to *never be late* for a meeting. I strongly agree with this rule. I.M. Boss did too, as long as it didn't pertain to him.

If one of us were ever late to a meeting, you would have thought we committed armed robbery against a family member. He would rant and rave for ten minutes or more about tardiness. However, he would be late for meetings about 75% of the time, sometimes keeping us waiting for thirty to forty–five minutes!

I.M. Boss was a poor example in other ways as well. In one instance, we were at a three–day corporate leadership conference out of town. These typically were about as much fun as getting wisdom teeth pulled.

I.M. Boss had an appointment scheduled with one of our large clients, which would pull him away from the last half day of meetings. The day before, our client called to cancel the meeting. I.M. Boss told me the next day just before leaving, "Our client cancelled on me but don't say anything to anyone, because I am still out of here. Have fun while I'm gone."

Now that is real leadership! That would be the same as a parent calling in sick to work while their kids are in the room and turning around to them and saying, "Don't tell anyone, but I am going to go play golf."

LEADERSHIP BY EXAMPLE

In a recent survey (from Ajilon Professional Staffing), I read that the single trait most desired in a boss is that they *lead by example* (according to 26% of respondents). Second most important is that they have *strong ethics and morals* (20%). In my opinion these two characteristics are very similar. If you lead by example, you should be doing so with high morals and ethics. So almost half of all respondents rated as their biggest desire for their bosses to have *high integrity and to lead by example.*

I challenge you to find anywhere in the Bible where Jesus wanted something for His own selfish reasons. You may say that that is not a fair comparison as Jesus didn't have to face what you and I face everyday. I beg to differ.

Did Jesus face tough temptations? You bet He did.

Picture yourself going without food for forty days. Do you think you would be hungry? Do you think you would eat something, even if it meant sinning?

Jesus had been fasting for forty days and nights (Matthew

4:2) when Satan appeared to Him in the desert. Where do you think Satan tempted Him? You're right, at His point of greatest weakness, His stomach.

Satan says, *"If you are the Son of God, tell these stones to become bread."* (Matthew 4:3)

Jesus' mouth had to be watering at the very thought. Finally, some food! However, Jesus knew that He was to remain above sin so He resisted by saying, *"It is written: 'Man does not live on bread alone, but on every word that comes from the mouth of God.'"* (Matthew 4:4)

Satan then decided to tempt Jesus' sense of pride by using Scripture himself:

> *Then the devil took him to the holy city and had him stand of the highest point of the temple. "If you are the Son of God," he said, "throw yourself down. For it is written: 'He will command his angels concerning you, and they will fly up in their hands, so that you will not strike your foot against a stone.'"*
>
> *Jesus answered him, "It is also written: 'Do not put the Lord your God to the test.'"*
>
> (Matthew 4:5–7)

Satan, now facing strike three, took Jesus to a high mountaintop and tried to appeal to Jesus' sense of entitlement. He showed Jesus all of the kingdoms of the world and said,

> *"All this I will give you if you will bow down and worship me."*
>
> *Jesus said to him, "Away from me Satan! For it is written, 'Worship the Lord your God, and serve him only.'"*

"Then the devil left him, and angels came and attended to him."

(Matthew 4:9–11)

Jesus faced temptation like you and I will never see; yet He was as pure as was possible. He had no impure thoughts. He had no sin. He always did what was right. Jesus did not make decisions based on the outcome. He did not give in to "situational ethics." He did not compromise His values for His selfish reasons.

Let's look at another instance where Jesus instructed by His example. In Matthew 3:14, Jesus went to the Jordan River and asked John the Baptist to baptize Him. John looked at Jesus with disbelief and said, *"I need to be baptized by you, and do you come to me?"* In other words, John was saying, "I am not worthy to do this to you. Why don't you baptize me instead?" Jesus says, *"Let it be so now; it is proper for us to do this to fulfill all righteousness."* John consented and baptized Jesus.

Baptism is a public ritual to show that we are followers of Christ. At the time of John the Baptist, baptism was a sign that they had asked God for forgiveness of their sins. Jesus did not need to be baptized, as He had no sin. He was Christ. But He humbled Himself to set an example for each of us.

Shouldn't we be like that as leaders? I believe that God will test us in this area as leaders to make sure that we can handle more responsibility.

We need to rise to the test and lead by example. We can't have a different set of rules for us than we do for those we lead. Do you think a parent can really get the message across to their children about the dangers of smoking while a cigarette is dangling from their lips?

IT WAS NOT ONLY JESUS

If you are saying, "Okay Jim, that is a great story about Jesus avoiding temptation. He could have easily avoided it, because He *was* God."

I agree that He was God; however, Scripture tells us that Jesus came to this world as a man and was tempted just as we are. In fact He was probably tempted more so than any of us will ever be. But the bottom line is that He did *NOT* act on that temptation.

It was not only Jesus who resisted temptation. There are some other great examples of this throughout Scripture.

Do you remember Joseph? He faced perhaps one of the greatest temptations of men–women and lust. As was mentioned earlier, Joseph was a great leader. However, his story was not without some major valleys and temptations.

If you recall, Joseph was made the head of his master's house. While his master was away, his master's wife begged him to sleep with her. I am sure Joseph was very tempted but he knew he had a higher purpose. He said to her, *"How could I do such a wicked thing and sin against God?"* (Genesis 39:9)

She could take it no longer as she was used to getting her way. When she cornered him alone in the house, Joseph fled the house but left his cloak in her hand. She took his cloak as proof that he tried to rape her. When his master returned he angrily threw Joseph in prison.

Though Joseph was innocent, he ended up in prison anyway. Do you think he said, "If I was going to end up in prison anyway, I should have slept with her and at least enjoyed myself?" I don't think so. Joseph was confident that God was with him and he felt that God had greater things in store for him. Succumbing to temptation would have hurt his situation more.

He could have viewed his predicament as hopeless. However, he knew God was refining him for something greater. Joseph followed what is taught to us in Colossians 3:23, *"Whatever you do, work at it with all your heart, as working for the Lord, not for men."* He performed each small task that was given him in prison to the best of his ability and the warden soon noticed his positive attitude and work ethic. He was promoted to prison administrator. So even in prison, Joseph was still being a good example to all.

Then Pharaoh had the cupbearer and the baker imprisoned. While in prison, they both had dreams interpreted by Joseph showing that they would be released. Joseph told them that the cupbearer would be restored to his position but the baker would be killed. The cupbearer had promised Joseph to speak well of him when he got out, but he forgot.

Two years later, Pharaoh had a dream and the cupbearer remembered that Joseph could interpret dreams. Pharaoh sent for Joseph. When Pharaoh asked if he could interpret these dreams, Joseph replied, *"I cannot do it, but God will give Pharaoh the answer he desires."* (Genesis 41:16) Joseph totally deflected the credit and gave it to God. After successfully interpreting his dream, Joseph was appointed by Pharaoh to be in charge of all Egypt.

Pretty incredible! When faced with a similar question regarding your ability to perform, are any of you like me? If you are, you might answer, "I sure can!" thinking that *we* are in total control. However, remember, as leaders it is important to focus on who is really in control – God.

We talked earlier about Moses who was regarded as the greatest Jewish leader. I don't think it is a coincidence that Moses gave all the credit to God throughout the Exodus. When God gave him the power to part the Red Sea, which allowed them to escape from the Egyptians, Moses did not gloat or say how great he was. What did he do? He sang a song to praise God. (Exodus 15)

Andy Stanley sums it up well in his book, *The Next Generation Leader*, when he says:

> *Character is not essential to leadership. We all know leaders who have led large organizations and garnered the loyalty of many followers, and yet lacked character. They demonstrated courage and competency. They were clear in their directives. They may have even sought the advice of others. But they were not men and women who were known for doing what was right. It is not uncommon to hear accomplished leaders attribute their success to business practices and personal conduct that most people would consider reprehensible. And yet there they are, king or queen of the mountain – at least for the moment.*

> *As we discussed earlier, you can lead without character.* But character is what makes you a leader worth following. *Integrity is not necessary if your aspirations as a leader end with simply persuading people to follow you. But if at the end of the day your intent is for those who follow to respect you, integrity is a must. Your accomplishments as a leader will make your name known. Your character will determine what people associate with your name.*

> *Your gifts and determination may dictate your potential, but it is your character that will determine your legacy. You can create an enviable lifestyle by leveraging your leadership skills alone. But you cannot create an enviable life without giving serious attention to who you are on the inside.*

SHARON OR STEVE?

Sharon and Steve work with you and are both in final interviews to be your next boss.

Nobody in your office has a problem with Sharon as she gets her job done. She works very hard, however, she tends to be late for meetings and she doesn't always respond to messages. In addition, she regularly tells dirty jokes at work. While the jokes are funny, they are not very appropriate in the office environment.

Steve, on the other hand also works hard. He may not get the same results Sharon gets, but he treats everyone very professionally. You have never known him to be late for a meeting or to forget a commitment.

Based solely upon the characteristics listed above, I would say that Steve would be the best leader. How do you feel?

As leaders, we need not gloat about our achievements. We need to lead by example and deflect the credit. Just as children will mimic what their parents do rather than what they say, those we lead will notice our behavior before they hear what we are telling them.

This concept reminds me of something that my dear friend and mentor, the late John Savage used to say, "Let people learn of your qualities and achievements from someone else." Amen!

Put to death, therefore, whatever belongs to your earthly nature: sexual immorality, impurity, lust, evil desires and greed, which is idolatry. Because of these, the wrath of God is coming. You used to walk in these ways, in the life you once lived. But now you must rid yourselves of all such things as these: anger, rage, malice, slander, and filthy language from your lips.

Colossians 3:5–8

When a man makes a vow to the Lord or takes an oath to obligate himself by a pledge, he must not break his word but must do everything he said.

Numbers 30:2

Let the Lord judge the peoples. Judge me, O Lord, according to my righteousness, according to my integrity, O Most High.

Psalm 7:8

Lord, who may dwell in your sanctuary? Who may live on your holy hill? He whose walk is blameless and who does what is righteous, who speaks the truth from his heart and has no slander on his tongue, who does his neighbor no wrong and casts no slur on his fellow-man, who despises a vile man but honors those who fear the Lord, who keeps his oath even when it hurts, who lends money without usury and does not accept a bribe against the innocent. He who does these things will never be shaken.

Psalm 15

Finally, brothers, whatever is true, whatever is noble, whatever is right, whatever is pure, whatever is lovely, whatever is admirable – if anything is excellent or praiseworthy – think about such things.

Philippians 4:8

Better a poor man whose walk is blameless than a fool whose lips are perverse.

Proverbs 19:1

The righteous man leads a blameless life; blessed are his children after him.

Proverbs 20:7

But the noble man makes noble plans, and by noble deeds he stands.

Isaiah 32:8

"So you must obey them and do everything they tell you. But do not do what they do, for they do not practice what they preach."

Matthew 23:3

CHAPTER 9
CALM LEADERSHIP

"Nothing gives one person so much advantage over another as to remain cool and unruffled under all circumstances."
– Thomas Jefferson

"Progress however, of the best kind, is comparatively slow. Great results cannot be achieved at once; and we must be satisfied to advance in life as we walk, step by step."
– Samuel Smiles

"The twin killers of success are impatience and greed."
– Jim Rohn

"Unreasonable haste is the direct road to error."
– Jean Baptiste Moliere

"Adopt the pace of nature. The secret is patience. A bottle fills drop by drop."
– Max Steingart

One day a farmer's donkey fell deep into a well. The animal cried piteously for hours as the farmer tried to figure out what to do. Finally he decided the animal was too old and wasn't worth saving.

Since his well needed to be covered up anyway, he invited all his neighbors over to help him bury the donkey in the well. They all grabbed a shovel and began to shovel dirt into the well. At first, the donkey realized what was happening and cried horribly.

Then, to everyone's amazement, he quieted down and became calm. A few shovel loads later, the farmer finally looked down the well and was astonished at what he saw.

With every shovel of dirt that hit his back, the donkey was doing something amazing. He would shake it off and take a step up.

As the farmer's neighbors continued to shovel dirt on top of the animal, he would shake it off and step up. Pretty soon, everyone was amazed as the donkey stepped over the edge of the well and trotted off!

Life is going to shovel dirt on us – all kinds of dirt. The trick to getting out of the well is to shake it off and take a step up. Each of our troubles is a stepping–stone. We can get out of the deepest wells just by persevering and never giving up! Shake it off and take a step up!

One fateful Wednesday, our corporate CFO and vice president of finance came to our office. I.M. Boss began the meeting with a dialogue stating how good we had been doing since he had been president. The CFO bluntly interrupted, "I.M.

Boss, cut the crap. Just tell us why you aren't growing your business." The meeting got worse from there.

After I.M. Boss took a beating from corporate most of the day, he ordered us all together and let us have it. It seems that verbal beatings roll downhill.

He told us that we needed to do something and do something fast to show corporate that we were serious about making some changes. As mentioned earlier, he told me I had to cut ten of thirty–four people in the sales organization. When I questioned the logic of cutting salespeople when sales were down, I was immediately shut down, "Lange, don't worry about this. Just get sales up and we won't have to cut any more people!"

In the end, we let over thirty people go, some of them very good employees – all to make I.M. Boss *look good.* Corporate later questioned I.M. Boss on his decision to get rid of sales people when we needed more sales and he danced around it as best he could.

There were numerous other instances when I.M. Boss would get so upset when things were not going according to his plan that he would literally start breathing like an angry bull. We could see the veins in his neck bulging and his entire face would turn red. This was never a good sign. This usually preceded some hasty decision that proved to be very unwise.

Don't we all want a leader who is calm when the storms come? I know I do.

Earlier, we discussed how Jesus fed over five thousand people with only five loaves of bread and two fish. One of the amazing parts of this story is the fact that His disciples had to be absolutely "freaking out." They had to be thinking, "Jesus, we have all of these people here with no food. Hungry people can get rowdy. Mobs can get ugly. We could really get hurt . . . or worse! Just send these people away Jesus, before the scene gets really bad!"

As evening approached, the disciples came to him and said, "This is a remote place, and it's already getting late. Send the crowds away, so they can go to the villages and buy themselves some food."

(Matthew 14:15)

How would *you* respond in this situation? In all honesty, I would probably panic.

Jesus replied, "They do not need to go away. You give them something to eat."

"We have here only five loaves of bread and two fish," they answered.

"Bring them here to me," he said. And he directed the people to sit down on the grass. Taking the five loaves and the two fish and looking up to heaven, he gave thanks and broke the loaves. Then he gave them to the disciples, and the disciples gave them to the people. They all ate and were satisfied, and the disciples picked up twelve basketfuls of broken pieces that were left over. The number of those who ate was about five thousand men, besides women and children.

(Matthew 14:16–21)

You see, had Jesus lost his cool, this wonderful miracle might not have happened. How many miracles are we letting slip by us, simply because we become stressed and panicked and lose our faith?

I read a book not too long ago about a prison inmate who was on death row. He had days to live and the way the author wrote the book, I felt as if I were in this man's shoes. I really got a sense of what this man was thinking and what he was going through. I could actually feel his stress of knowing he was about to die, right up until the moment of his death!

Think about Jesus. He knew for years that He was destined to die at a young age. He also knew that He would die a most horrible death. He knew that He would suffer greatly.

The night before His impending death, Jesus was in great anguish. His human nature was coming through, as He wanted to avoid this pain. It had to be unbearable stress – enough for even Jesus to crack, I would think. But Jesus held fast to be a great example for all of us. He is definitely the epitome of a calm leader.

Then Jesus went with his disciples to a place called Gethsemane, and he said to them, "Sit here while I go over there and pray." He took Peter and the two sons of Zebedee along with him, and he began to be sorrowful and troubled. Then he said to them, "My soul is overwhelmed with sorrow to the point of death. Stay here and keep watch with me."

Going a little farther, he fell with his face to the ground and Prayed, "My Father, if it is possible, may this cup be taken from me. Yet not as I will, but as you will."
(Matthew 26:36–39)

Shortly after this, Jesus was betrayed by Judas and was arrested. How would you feel at this point? I would be absolutely terrified and would try to flee. I would at least want to hurt those who captured me. But not Jesus, He remained perfectly calm:

When Jesus' followers saw what was going to happen, they said, "Lord should we strike with our swords?"

And one of them struck the servant of the high priest,
cutting off his right ear.

But Jesus answered, "No more of this!" And he touched
the man's ear and healed him.

(Luke 22:49–51)

He not only remained calm, He actually healed one of His captors! Jesus knew, that to be a truly great leader, He needed to calmly do what was necessary to prove that He *was* the Son of God.

One of the greatest examples of Jesus' calm leadership came when He and His disciples were in a boat and a great storm arose.

Without warning, a furious storm came up on the lake,
so that the waves swept over the boat. But Jesus was
sleeping. The disciples went and woke him, saying,
"Lord save us! We're going to drown!" He replied,
"You of little faith, why are you so afraid?" Then he
got up and rebuked the winds and the waves, and it was
completely calm.

(Matthew 8:24–26)

Have you ever been on a boat where waves were coming over the side? It can be very frightening. Let's look at how Jesus reacted a little more closely.

What was He doing at this time? He was sleeping! Other than death, I challenge you to come up with a more calm state than sleeping. I think that Jesus *chose* to be sleeping at this time as He wanted to show us how at peace He really was, so that we could learn from Him.

When someone suddenly awakens you with a frantic voice, how do you respond? My heart pounds and I tend to get panicky and quickly look around to try to get my bearings. This text suggests that Jesus, simply and calmly responded by saying, "Chill out guys. Where is your faith? There is absolutely no need to worry. I, with my Father's help, have this totally under control."

How awesome it had to be for His disciples to witness that. That would certainly change my way of thinking when it came to crisis management!

Now, I am not suggesting that we can merely raise our hands and stop the hurricane that is happening in our business or home lives. I am also not suggesting that we should sleep during the storms of our lives. However, we do have the ability the voice of reason during turbulent times. Wouldn't you rather follow someone who is being calm during the storm than the one who is panicking? I think those that follow us feel the same way.

SHARON OR JOHN?

Sharon and John are coworkers of yours and are the final candidates to become your new boss.

Sharon works very hard and is always busy. She performs well when there are no unanticipated interruptions in her day. When those do occur, however, she totally loses focus, is noticeably stressed and does not perform well.

John also is a hard worker but is much more easy going. He seems to realize that "stuff" will happen throughout the day, which will cause him to get off track. He takes these setbacks in stride and simply goes about his business.

Based only on the above information, John would clearly be the most qualified to be leader of your department as he would be more likely to provide calm leadership in the midst of the everyday storms.

A hot–tempered man stirs up dissension, but a patient man calms a quarrel.

Proverbs 15:18

If a ruler's anger rises against you, do not leave your post; calmness can lay great errors to rest.

Ecclesiastes 10:4

A fool gives full vent to his anger, but a wise man keeps himself under control.

Proverbs 29:11

CHAPTER 10

SO WHAT DO WE DO NOW?

"The difference between a successful
person and others is not a lack of strength, not a
lack of knowledge, but rather in a lack of will."
– Vince Lombardi

"One person with a belief is equal to a force
of ninety–nine with only interests."
– John Stuart Mill

"You can do anything in life you set your mind
to, provided it is powered by your heart."
– Doug Firebaugh

"To grow, you must be willing to let your present and future
be totally unlike your past. Your history is not your destiny."
– Alan Cohen

"Always do the best we can. This is our
sacred human responsibility."
– Albert Einstein

THE RIPPLE

Drop a pebble in the water, just a splash, and it's gone;
But there's half–a–hundred ripples circling on and on and on,
Spreading, spreading from the center, flowing out to the sea,
And there is no way of telling where the end is going to be.

Drop a pebble in the water: in a minute you forget,
But there's little waves a – flowing, and here's ripples circling yet,
And those little waves a flowing to a reat big wave have grown;
You've disturbed a mighty river just by dropping a stone.

Drop an unkind word, or careless: in a minute it is gone;
But there's half–a–hundred ripples circling on and on and on,
They keep spreading, spreading, spreading from the center they a go,
And there is no way to stop them, once you've started them to flow.

Drop an unkind word, or careless: in a minute you forget;
But there's little waves a – flowing, and there's ripples circling yet,
And perhaps in some sad heart a mighty wave of tears you've stirred;
And disturbed a life was happy ere you dropped that unkind word.

Drop a word of cheer and kindness: just a splash and it's gone;
But there's half–a–hundred ripples circling on and on and on,
Bearing hope and joy and comfort on each splashing, dashing wave,
'Till you wouldn't believe the volume of the one kind word you gave.

Drop a word of cheer and kindness: in a minute you forget;
But there's gladness still a – swelling, and there's joy a – circling yet,
And you've rolled a wave of comfort whose sweet music can be heard,
Over miles and miles of water just by dropping one kind word.

~ James W. Foley

══════════════════════════════════════

　　While much of the content of this book is common sense,
it never ceases to amaze me that it is so widely *not* followed in

corporate America. My hope and prayer is that this book has touched you in some way and given you the desire to be the best leader you can be.

One of our family's favorite movies is Disney's *The Lion King*. In the movie, Simba, who is heir to the throne of the kingdom, leaves the kingdom because of some guilt he was hanging on to. Later, a baboon named Rafiki finds him and asks him to come back to rule over the kingdom, as he is desperately needed.

Simba tells Rafiki that he *was* heir to the throne in the past but the past does not matter – it is too painful for him to go back and resume his duties. Rafiki proceeds to swat him over the head with his large stick.

Simba says, "Ouch, what did you do that for?!"

Rafiki answers, "It doesn't matter, it is in the past."

"Yeah, but it hurt!" Simba replies.

Rafiki then swings his stick again and Simba ducks. Rafiki says, "Ah, but you *learned* from your past!"

If you have read this and realized that you have been less than a good leader, *don't worry.* Even if looking back on your career is a painful experience, remember Rafiki's lesson above. Even though the past can hurt, we all can learn from it and we can improve on it.

The bottom line is that we are all less than perfect. Even the greatest of leaders in the Bible, other than Jesus, were far from perfect. So don't beat yourself up if you have not been a model leader in the past. Someone once said that the difference between a winner and a loser is that *the winner has failed more often.*

The past does not have to equal the future. God created each of us to succeed. Today truly is the first day of the rest of your life. Why not decide that you will make these characteristics a part of who you are?

BIBLICAL CHARACTERISTICS OF A LEADER

- Humility

- Compassion

- Servant–hood

- Forgiveness

- A Good Listener

- Inclusiveness

- Integrity

- Calmness

I encourage you to remember this when leading *your* flock. They need you to lead like our Biblical leaders, especially Christ.

It all begins in your mind. You have to want to be a great leader. You have to think you can. We must lead by example.

If you think you are beaten, you are,
If you think you dare, you don't,
If you like to win, but you think you can't,
It is almost certain you won't.

If you think you'll lose, you're lost
For out of the world we find,
Success begins with a fellow's will
It's all in the state of mind.

If you think you are outclassed, you are,
You've got to think high to rise,
You've got to be sure of yourself before
You can ever win a prize.

Life's battles don't always go
To the stronger or faster of man,
But soon or late, the man who wins
Is the one WHO THINKS HE CAN!!!

– Napoleon Hill –

But the fruit of the Spirit is love, joy, peace, patience,
kindness, goodness, faithfulness, gentleness and self–
control. Against such things there is no law.
                                    Galatians 5:22-23

Jesus replied: "'Love the Lord your God with all your
heart and with all your soul and with all your mind.'
This is the first and greatest commandment. And the
second is like it: 'Love your neighbor as yourself.' All
the Law and the Prophets hang on these two command-
ments."
                                    Matthew 22:37 – 39

Appendix A –

How to Have Everlasting Life

*For it is by grace you have been saved, through faith
– and this not from yourselves, it is the gift of God – not
by works, so that no one can boast.*

(Ephesians 2:8–9)

For the first thirty–six years of my life, I thought that I
needed to be "good" to go to heaven. That simply is not true. The
apostle Paul tells us in Ephesians (shown above) that it has nothing to do with our "works" or deeds. It is simply a matter of our
faith in Jesus Christ, believing that He is our Lord and Savior.

The bottom line is that we have *all* sinned – *for all have
sinned and fall short of the glory of God.* (Romans 3:23)

Sinning does not bode well for our future – *For the wages
of sin is death, but the gift of God is eternal life in Christ Jesus
our Lord.* (Romans 6:23)

We have a chance, though. We can die to our sins and
start new – *"I tell you the truth, no one can see the kingdom of
God unless he is born again."* (John 3:3)

* I have to admit that the term "born again" used to freak
me out. I thought that meant that you dressed up in robes, shaved
your head and were generally a freak. However, it simply means
that you have a new spiritual birthday – a fresh start with Christ.

Jesus tells us how we do this – *Jesus answered, "I am the
way and the truth and the life. No one comes to the Father except
through me."* (John 14:6)

Further instruction – *That if you confess with your mouth,
"Jesus is Lord," and believe in your heart that God raised him
from the dead, you will be saved.* (Romans 10:9)

This is good news for us – *"For God so loved the world that he gave his one and only Son, that whoever believes in him shall not perish but have eternal life."* (John 3:16)

All we need to do is ask and Jesus will be with us – *"Here I am! I stand at the door and knock. If anyone hears my voice and opens the door, I will come in and eat with him, and he with me."* (Revelation 3:20)

If you have not invited Jesus into your heart to be Lord of your life, I invite you to read this prayer:

"Dear Lord, I want to know you. I want you to be Lord of my life. I am willing, with your help, to turn from my sins. Thank you for sending Jesus to die on the cross for my sins. Thank you for allowing Him to rise again to be my Savior. Come into my life and show me the way." Amen.

If this prayer expresses what you feel in your heart, I encourage you to read aloud the prayer above, or something similar, to begin a personal relationship with God.

What happens when you receive Christ as your Savior?

• Jesus comes into your life.

(Revelation 3:20)

• You become a child of God.

(John 1:12)

• Your sins are forgiven.

(Colossians 1:14)

• You have eternal life.

(I John 5:11–13)

• You begin the adventure of knowing God personally.
(Philippians 3:8)

WHAT'S NEXT?

• Talk to God about everything in prayer.

(Philippians 4:6–7)

• Listen to God by reading the Bible.

(Hebrews 4:12)

• Spend time with others who know God personally in fellowship.

(Hebrews 10:25)

• Help others to know God personally.

(Matthew 28:19–20)

• Let God direct your life everyday.

(John 14:15)

Contact Jim Lange at
www.bleedership.com

or order more copies of this book at

TATE PUBLISHING, LLC

127 East Trade Center Terrace
Mustang, Oklahoma 73064

(888) 361 – 9473

Tate Publishing, LLC

www.tatepublishing.com